John L. Porter

Naval Constructor of Destiny

John L. Porter
1831–1893

John L. Porter

Naval Constructor of Destiny

Alan B. Flanders

BRANDYLANE PUBLISHERS, INC.
White Stone, Virginia

in cooperation with
the Friends of the Portsmouth Naval Shipyard Museum, Inc.

 Brandylane Publishers, Inc.

P.O. Box 261, White Stone, Virginia 22578
(804) 435-6900 or 1 800 553-6922; e-mail: brandy@crosslink.net

Copyright 2000, by Alan B. Flanders
All rights reserved
Printed in the United States of America

Library of Congress Cataloging-in-Publication Data

Flanders, Alan B.
    John L. Porter: naval constructor of destiny / Alan Flanders.
      p. cm.
    Includes bibliographical references and index.
    ISBN 1-883911-40-0
    1. Porter, John L. (John Luke), 1813– 2. Naval architects—Virginia—Biography. I. Title.

VM140.P7 F56 2000
623.8'1'092—dc21
[B]   00–022114

It is an honor to dedicate this book to the volunteer docents of the Portsmouth Naval Shipyard Museum, Portsmouth, Virginia. Because of their generous donation of time and resources, the maritime history of Portsmouth has been preserved.

CONTENTS

Acknowledgments	*viii*
Introduction	*ix*
Life on the Elizabeth	1
The Pittsburgh Proposal	7
Saving a Wooden Hull Treasure: Rebuilding the USS *Constellation*	15
Yellow Fever Epidemic	19
Politics, Prayers and Steam Frigates	21
On the Brink at Pensacola	25
In the Middle of a Civil War	31
Home to Portsmouth	37
The Stage Is Set: The Burning of Gosport	41
Ironclad Decision	53
In His Own Words: The CSS *Virginia*	63
Porter vs. Brooke: The Public Debate	73
Battle of Hampton Roads	89
Building a Confederate Navy	99
The CSS *Richmond*	107
A Hotbed of Politics	113
The Long Way Home	119
A True Rendering	127
Bibliography	*133*
Index	*139*

ACKNOWLEDGMENTS

First and foremost, I would once again like to thank the Friends of the Portsmouth Naval Shipyard Museum, Portsmouth, Virginia, for their generosity in publishing this book. Without their continued interest in preserving local and national maritime history through publications, books like this would not be possible.

I would also like to thank the staff of the Portsmouth Naval Shipyard Museum for their steadfast help during the writing of this book. As always, their encouragement, research assistance and general support were a tremendous help in making the writing and editing of the manuscript a pleasure.

Since I began my research into the life of John L. Porter, his descendants have continued to provide a vast collection of previously unpublished primary documents, memoirs and family stories that comprise a good portion of this book. Since it was my intention to allow the subject of this work, John L. Porter, to speak for himself as much as possible, especially concerning the conversion of the USS *Merrimac(k)* into the ironclad CSS *Virginia*, the Porter family's contributions were invaluable in understanding the complex times of this remarkable character. Recognizing that historians would be interested in John L. Porter's own words about the history of the CSS *Virginia*, his memoirs, for the first time, are published in their entirety. In many ways this is John L. Porter's book.

INTRODUCTION

A Life of Historical Ironies

John Luke Porter's life began on September 19, 1813, during a second war with Great Britain in which the United States emerged as a recognized naval power. The irony at the beginning of Porter's life was that he would spend a good portion of his time as a naval constructor making obsolete those famous wooden hulls of the War of 1812.

From his family background and considerable natural talent, it was not surprising, to those who knew him, that he should have become a notable ship constructor. Given the Porter family tradition of public service and religious toleration, that he was a highly influential leader in the Methodist Church and first president of Portsmouth's city council surprised no one. The fact that he first conceived the idea of building an ironclad warship as early as 1846 and was then ignored by a fraternity of wooden-hull sailing ship admirals was not surprising. Looking back, it could have been no surprise that 15 years later he went on to design and build the world's first battle-tested ironclad warship to see combat against another ironclad. But it is again ironical that Porter did not seek a patent on his invention since he felt the *Virginia* was not seaworthy and only valuable for harbor defense.

That he was firmly against secession and favored the abolition of slavery is enlightening, but again predictable for a man who "lived" his religion. He read his bible daily, taught Sunday school, conducted church meetings at his house and held daily bible readings with his fellow shipyard workers as often as time allowed. He could have easily been mistaken for a clergyman with his quiet ways that allowed for deep thought, introspection, and humility. However, national events drew him down a far different path. It literally took the Civil War to force him to reluctantly turn from a highly successful career in the United States Navy and cast his lot with his community and state in what he knew was an impracticable and unrealistic act of secession from the Union. Despite his frank appraisal from the beginning of war that his chosen side would probably lose, he still gave all of his

Introduction

considerable talent to the development of the Confederate Navy. That is indeed another irony in John L. Porter's life.

Porter's background reveals a portrait of a very complex and gifted man at once at the pinnacle of his career, and then lost in the debacle of the Confederacy's defeat and the harsh reconstruction that followed.

Yet, he remains an obscure figure in the annals of American naval history, and that is the final irony. Hopefully, those who read this story of his life will agree that he now deserves his rightful place in that history as one of America's most gifted ship constructors, whose achievements did indeed change the course of world naval history forever.

Porter had inherited and developed not only a natural genius in ship design and construction, but he had also inherited and developed strong personality traits of loyalty and fidelity from one of the nation's most distinguished and oldest families.

As he grew up in Portsmouth, Virginia, along the Elizabeth River, during the first two decades of the 19th century, he was made aware of family civic responsibility and dedication to public service as well as a long tradition of Porter shipbuilding. As a young man, Porter found solace in his family's active spiritual life, which played a major role in his adulthood. Although the Porters were members of established churches, Anglican (later Episcopal) and Methodist, his colonial forebear, John Porter, had strongly and openly supported religious tolerance for Quakers during a time of intolerance.

Military service was another dominant theme in the Porter family. Porter's grandfather, William Porter, Jr., was a soldier in the Revolutionary War. Breaking from his Tory neighbors, he entered the army in 1775, as a lieutenant in the 12th Virginia Regiment, was promoted to captain of an artillery company, and served with distinction until the close of the war. He was also a vestryman in the "Established Church" and filled a number of official positions in Norfolk County. In 1782, William Porter, Jr. married Elizabeth Luke, hence the origin of John Luke Porter's middle name, although he usually signed his name "John L. Porter." Elizabeth Luke was the daughter of famed ship carver Isaac Luke, and a cousin of Revolutionary War naval hero Commodore Richard Dale. John Luke Porter's father, Joseph

Introduction

Porter, served as captain of Virginia troops during the War of 1812.

Local history records that John L. Porter was a direct descendant of John Porter, Jr. who settled in what was then Norfolk County in the early 1600's. He married Mary Sidney, daughter of Colonel John Sidney of the colonial militia and became one of the justices of the Norfolk County Court and High Sheriff of the county as well. John Porter, Jr. was followed by Samuel Porter who died in 1698, Samuel Porter, Jr., 1718, William Porter, 1760, William Porter, Jr., 1807, and Joseph Porter, father of John Luke Porter, who died in 1831. Commercial records of the time indicate that both William Porter, Jr. and Joseph Porter owned and operated small shipyards adjacent to Gosport shipyard, a former Royal Navy shipyard that was later purchased from the Commonwealth of Virginia by the federal government after it was confiscated during the Revolution. Before establishing their shipyard, the Porters were active in the merchant trade between the Virginia colony and London.

It was from this heritage that John L. Porter derived his personal traits of honesty, spiritual strength, humility and genius. It is the purpose of this biography to recreate a portrait of John L. Porter that accurately reveals these traits.

CHAPTER ONE

Life on the Elizabeth

When John L. Porter first told his father Joseph Porter II, a master shipbuilder and owner of a prominent Portsmouth shipyard, that he would like to follow him in the profession of ship construction, the senior Porter was elated. It was his plan that his youngest son would rise from his apprenticeship to take over the management of the Porter shipyard.

Just down the Elizabeth River from the growing Gosport shipyard complex, Joseph Porter had pioneered work on not only sailing vessels but early steamboats as well. In fact the Porter shipyard had helped pioneer steam propulsion in the South. Now the Porters would make their name not only as one of Virginia's founding families in law and politics, but also in shipbuilding.

Even though contemporary accounts of the Joseph Porter shipyard are rare, surviving newspaper articles describe its capacity. The earliest story in an April 3, 1812 edition of the *Herald,* noted that Joseph Porter was then in partnership with William Dyson on the Portsmouth side of the Elizabeth River. The article proudly announced the launch of "a ship called the *Indian Chief,* constructed by Messrs. Dyson and Porter. The exhibition drew together a large and respectable concourse of the citizens of Norfolk and Portsmouth, all anxious to behold a scene so congenial to the spirit of commercial enterprize . . ."

The publicity and growing prominence of the Porter yard were no doubt good news for Porter's growing family that included Caroline, William, Sidney, Virginia, Emily, Joseph, Fletcher,

Angelina, and the youngest, John L. Porter.

By March 1820, however, the partnership with Dyson was dissolved. Joseph Porter bought Dyson's remaining share of the yard and continued it on his own. Meanwhile Dyson moved down river to begin his business in competition with his former partner.

During John L. Porter's youth, he was no doubt exposed to the considerable talents of naval constructor Francis Grice whose reputation was known and respected along the entire eastern seaboard as the successor of famed shipbuilders Joshua Humphreys and Josiah Fox. The 1820 launch of the 74-gun USS *Delaware* from Gosport shipyard brought international attention to Gosport shipyard as a national leader in warship construction. During this time, Porter was able to serve for a time as Grice's apprentice. However, his father's shipyard no doubt kept him busy in the carpentry trade as well. A July 22, 1829, *Herald* article described Joseph Porter's shipyard as eager to get into the canal boat building business that must have tested the younger Porter's physical endowments in his father's workshop.

"Now on the Stocks, and can be launched in 12 or 15 days, a Vessel constructed for the canal business and likewise for coasting. The model of this vessel differs materially from any that has been built for that purpose in the port of Norfolk. Persons wishing to purchase such a vessel are invited to call at the Ship Yard of the Subscriber, and examine for themselves, as respects the model, materials and workmanship of said vessel. The dimensions are 61 feet keel; 16 feet three inches beam; 5 feet depth, from beam to sealing. Joseph Porter."

Just how advanced Joseph Porter's shipyard was in steam engineering for its day is portrayed in an article in the May 18th, 1827 *Herald* which announced the launch of the steamboat *Fredericksburg*. "A steam vessel of 180 tons burthen, was launched yesterday in handsome style, from the ship yard of Mr. JOSEPH PORTER, in Portsmouth. She is called the *Fredericksburg,* and is intended to run between Washington and Potomac Creek; was built under the superintendence of Mr. William Lambell, of Washington, and is pronounced to be an elegant vessel in every respect, supporting the well earned reputation of Mr. Porter as a ship builder."

No doubt John L. Porter was proud of the *Fredericksburg*, as she became a very prominent advertisement for the Porter enterprise when she began regular calls at Norfolk in March 1832. That same month, the *Herald* advertised for the Porters by describing the *Fredericksburg* as "a swift and good boat, with a low pressure engine, and her accommodations for passengers and freight such as it is hoped will give satisfaction to those who may be inclined to patronize the undertaking." However, as fate would have it, John L. Porter had to shoulder responsibilities as a family leader early in his career.

When his father became too ill to run the shipyard, the family was forced to sell the business and their family home. The family resources were further limited when Fletcher Porter was discovered to be blind in one eye. After Joseph Porter died in August, 1831, at the age of 48, an 18-year old John L. Porter and his brother Joseph H. were faced with the responsibility of supporting not only their mother, but Fletcher and their other siblings as well. Realizing they could make a living first with their hands, they offered their trade as carpenters to a number of other shipbuilding concerns along the Elizabeth, including Gosport, to support the family. Fortunately, Fletcher Porter would maintain his sight well into adulthood during which he earned a reputation as a very talented carpenter before going completely blind. Later, Unionist members of Monumental Methodist Church presented Fletcher Porter with one of the first raised-letter bibles in the South. Meanwhile Joseph H. Porter permanently joined Gosport shipyard and worked for the United States Navy as a Master Block and Gun Carriage maker where he would rise to political prominence.

Fortunately, Porter's daughter, Martha Buxton (Porter) Brent, wrote an extensive memoir at Wakefield, Virginia in July 1934, that in part offers some perspective about this period that otherwise would not have been available. According to the Brent memoir, despite financial problems caused by the loss of her grandfather and the family shipyard, Porter had begun a courtship with "the belle of Nansemond County, Susan Naylor Buxton." In September 1834, at 21-years old, Porter married Susan Buxton, then 17, and the two began their family at the Court Street home of Isaac Luke in Portsmouth. In the Luke home, which was also now the residence of his mother, all of Porter's children would be born including George, Mary Susan, Alice, John W.H., and Martha Buxton (Brent), with the exception of James Buxton, who would arrive later in Washington, DC. But according to Brent, the newlyweds soon faced further financial problems.

"About this time my father and uncle Sidney undertook a business venture which failed utterly," wrote Brent. "There was quite a trade between Norfolk and the West Indies, and their plan was to build a brig to run between these two points, and make a good deal, carrying freight back and forth. My father borrowed the money from cousin Willis and Uncle Joe Moore, and as they were both masters of shipbuilding, he and uncle Sidney put out a substantial, well-built brig.

"She was loaded and started on her first voyage, but a terrible storm arose. She must have been badly handled, anyhow she went to the bottom on her first trip, leaving my father the weight of the debt, for my uncle went off to Alabama."

Subsequently Porter took work wherever he could find it to pay off the debt. Fortunately, he could fall back on his ship's carpentry skills and found employment not only in the government-owned Gosport shipyard, but in a number of private yards as well. He got along well with the owners and master carpenters of these smaller, private yards, which would come in handy later in the Civil War. His skills both in design and practical mechanics and carpentry were becoming well known throughout the Hampton Roads area.

It was during this period that Porter decided to leave the ship carpenter's shop for the constructor's office. From his youth he had evidenced a natural skill in mechanical drawing and understanding of ship design and construction. From watching the introduction of steam power on the Elizabeth and the building of steam plants in several of his father's ships, he knew that soon steam and iron would replace sail and wood. For Porter, the future was beckoning in the North where advancements in iron construction and steam engineering were already a reality.

Porter met and befriended U.S. Navy engineer Lieutenant William W. Hunter whose novel experiments with submerged paddle wheels on the Elizabeth River captured headlines around the world. Shortly after their meeting, Hunter, who became a lifelong friend, and for whom Porter named his fourth child John

William Hunter Porter, played a prominent role in obtaining government work for Porter.

"My father said he would turn around the corner any time to keep from meeting either of his creditors; that he would have been glad to see Judgement Day come," recalled Brent. "However, he shouldered the debt, like the honest man that he was; they lived plainly and hired out the slaves. My mother wore calico dresses to church, and finally, there came a day when cousin Willis and Uncle Joe were invited to dine, and the last of the debt was paid and the receipts given and my dear father breathed freely again. He had learned his lesson. He would not even have a book at a grocery store, nor go in debt for a week's provisions. I don't think thereafter that he ever went in debt for ten dollars."

CHAPTER TWO

The Pittsburgh Ironclad Plan of 1846

"I think it was somewhere in the early forties (1842) that my father moved to Pittsburgh with his family to build a vessel (USS *Allegheny*) for the Government. There were four children," Brent wrote.

"It was while in Pittsburgh that my father offered to the Government his plan of an ironclad war ship, but they apparently thought little of the invention, or thought it would never be needed. Anyway, they declined to consider it."

The "Porter plan for an ironclad bombproof-1846" has been the subject of some scholarly speculation and controversy ever since. However, there seems little doubt today that Porter did devise a plan in 1846 to apply armor plating to a steam-driven warship and discussed it with Lieutenant Hunter during their work on the *Allegheny*. Eminent Harvard University naval historian James M. Baxter mentioned the plan in his authoritative treatise, *The Introduction of the Ironclad Warship*.

"John L. Porter had been employed by the United States Navy Department, at the request of Lieutenant William W. Hunter, in the construction of the unsuccessful iron steamers *Water Witch* and *Allegheny*," wrote Baxter. "In his (Porter's) article dated October, 1887, in Battles and Leaders of the Civil War, he (Porter) stated that in April, 1846, while superintending the construction of the latter ship at Pittsburgh, he (Porter) 'conceived the idea of an iron-clad, and made a model with the exact shield which I (Porter) placed on the *Merrimac*.' According to Porter's son, John

William Hunter Porter, the 1846 plan called for an iron vessel of nineteen feet draft and forty feet beam, whose sides sloped inward at an angle of 45 degrees from the knuckle, which was two feet below the water line. Three inches of inclined armor covering 'all of the vessel above the water line and to a depth of four feet below it,' the designer deemed sufficient to withstand the heaviest ordnance of the day."

J.W.H. Porter wrote that the 1846 model was to be equipped with Hunter's submersible wheels and had a protected ironclad gun deck that ran literally the full length of the vessel, three feet above the water line. J.W.H. Porter added that, "The protective shield in which the battery was located was built in the middle of the ship. The ends beyond the shield were constructed upon the same incline, as to their sides, as the shield, and the deck forward and aft of the shield was protected with armor plate." The 1846 plan also required wrought-iron port shutters. "The resisting surface was to have been entirely of iron," noted J.W.H. Porter.

Baxter wrote that, "On examining those plans, Lieutenant Hunter suggested the adoption of an iron protective deck, to be built below the gun deck, for added protection against the plunging fire. Porter added this feature to his drawings, and dispatched them to the Navy Department, which took no further notice of them than to acknowledge their receipt, but Mr. Porter transferred them to his book of naval designs which he retained and still has in his possession."

Although Baxter acknowledges the plan, he added that, "A careful search in the archives of the Navy Department and of the Bureau of Construction and Repair has failed to reveal these plans, or any reference to them in the correspondence of Hunter and Porter with either the Department or the Bureau." Porter apparently felt some rebuke at the Department's lack of interest in his novel idea and simply entered them into his notebook where they remain today. It is important to remember that several times during his construction of the ironclad CSS *Virginia*, he made reference to the 1846 concept, as did others in official capacity. There is now no dispute among naval historians that he adapted many of its characteristics during the conversion of the steam frigate USS *Merrimac(k)* into the CSS *Virginia*.

At any rate, among his other duties at Pittsburgh, Porter began to study for the Navy Department's naval constructor examination. In the autumn of 1847, he traveled to the Washington Navy Yard and took the test without passing marks. However, he subsequently passed and was officially appointed U.S. Naval Constructor.

Although the 1846-plan never became a reality, Porter's first major achievement, the iron-hulled *Allegheny* did. Measuring 185 feet in length and carrying a beam of over 33 feet and requiring a draft of 13 feet, 6 inches, Porter designed her to carrying four 8-inch smooth bore cannons.

Lieutenant Hunter, Porter's partner at the Tomlinson Shipyard, Pittsburgh, supervised the addition of his "Hunter Wheels" for *Allegheny*'s propulsion system.

Unfortunately for Porter and Hunter, the *Allegheny* was to be an unlucky ship beset by mechanical problems that steered her away from fame and into the breaking yards. She was launched from Tomlinson Shipyard with the usual fanfare as the newly commissioned ship constructor John L. Porter and Lieutenant Hunter looked on. Her brief history in the *Dictionary of American Naval Fighting Ships* records a rather lackluster performance.

From Pittsburgh she steamed on to serve on the Brazilian Station, followed by duty in the Mediterranean in 1848, and tours in the Gulf of Mexico in 1849. During her final cruise, the Hunter Wheels began to cause serious problems. She was later laid up in 1851-1852 in Portsmouth, Virginia's A. Mehaffy shipyard where the Hunter Wheels were switched out for a screw propeller.

For a moment in 1852 there was a glimmer of hope for the *Allegheny*. Commodore M.C. Perry's expedition was being formed in Hampton Roads for its historic cruise to Japan and *Allegheny* was selected to join the flotilla. However, she failed the preliminary tests and was subsequently taken off the active list and placed in ordinary at the Washington Navy Yard. In 1856 she was converted into a receiving ship and sent to the Baltimore, Maryland waterfront where she rotted away during the Civil War. Badly in need of overhaul, she was sent down the Chesapeake to Norfolk, Virginia once more. Due to the over abundance of ships under repair from the war, she was stricken from the active list and sold for scrap at Norfolk in May 1869.

Unfortunately for Porter, his first ship would come back to

haunt him as a derelict on the Elizabeth River after the Civil War.

While Porter was busily engaged in shipbuilding at Pittsburgh, his brother, Joseph H. was busy building the family's political name back in Portsmouth at Gosport. On August 20, 1842, Joseph H. Porter chaired a meeting of the yard mechanics during which the debate about whether the yard should be under civilian or military control reached a boiling point. A strong current of racial tension between white and black workers further fueled the controversy.

Under Joseph H. Porter's leadership, the mechanics formally petitioned the shipyard commander for complete control over the construction and repair of U.S. Navy vessels. Furthermore, the mechanics cited interference from U.S. Naval officers during shipbuilding and repairs and asked the yard commander to restrict the officers from any supervisory power during any further yard work. Joseph H. Porter wrote in the minutes of the meeting, which were later published in the August 25th, 1842 *Beacon,* that, "The interests of the country would be promoted, and the condition of those employed in the Public Yards ameliorated, by divesting Officers of the Navy of the power of controlling the mechanical operations in the various yards, and in lieu thereof, confiding the management of those concerns to competent Civil Officers, we consider it our duty to petition Congress to the effect aforesaid." It is probable that Porter's recording secretary, John Jack, added to the article by writing a letter in support of the Mechanic's petition that served to strengthen racial tensions that would of course soon come to the forefront. The letter, signed by "A Practical Mechanic," stated, "The fact that a man is a commodore, commander or Lieutenant, does not substantiate the fact or proposition that he is competent to direct the building of a ship, no more than it does that a carpenter, smith or boat builder, is fully equal to the task of sailing or of fighting one." The letter goes on to read, "Nor do they wish to see Negro laborers substituted for white mechanics, when they know, and those who are guilty of so gross a piece of injustice likewise know, if they are as competent as they pretend, that the change is a positive loss to the government."

By 1850, Porter had returned to Portsmouth and the

tranquillity of domestic life. In the Brent memoir, he is remembered as a choir leader, like his father and brother George, at the Monumental Methodist Church. In fact both Porter and his brother George entertained their families in the parlor with music on Sunday afternoons. Brent described how she and the rest of the family would gather while her brother George entertained them. "I remember very distinctly sitting on a little footstool and listening with delight to his singing and playing on the guitar." No doubt Porter took great pride in his son's musical abilities. It was also during this period that Porter began to seriously follow in the political footsteps of his family and take part in the political leadership of Portsmouth.

In its centennial year, 1852, Portsmouth's Board of Trustees was replaced by a mayor and city council. Subsequently the town was divided into two wards. Gosport and everything east of Court and Fourth Streets near the Gosport Shipyard were designated as the Jackson Ward, with the remainder called the Jefferson Ward. Porter was a popular figure in both voting sections with his brother, Joseph H. Porter helping to turn out support from Gosport, and leaders from Monumental Methodist getting the Jefferson Ward to support him as well. Normally reserved, and at times painfully quiet, Porter must have been the very person voters were looking for as he won an overwhelming victory. Brent wrote, "In 1852 Portsmouth was incorporated as a Town. My father, John L. Porter, was President of the first common council."

During this time, the issue of slavery once again became a source of national debate. As a devout Christian, Porter was against the institution of slavery, although he had inherited slaves from his father. However, Porter planned to free them before the Civil War. The Brent memoir contains a family incident that reveals how close the Porters were to their slaves.

"About 1854 my father had saved enough money to buy a piano for my oldest sister (Mary Susan), and she was very happy in the prospect of music lessons from a professor in the fall, but tragedy occurred in the life of the colored members of our family that brought her a great disappointment.

"There were very few slaves in my father's family. His

11

grandfather (William Porter), a very wealthy man, set all his slaves free by his will, as soon as they should reach the age of twenty-one. But my mother inherited slaves, among them a man, Willis Hodges, by name, of whom my father and mother thought a great deal, and all the children loved him.

"Willis had married a woman named Matilda, a slave of Colonel Binford, a prominent, wealthy man of Portsmouth. Matilda and Willis had three children, when Colonel Binford died. Here arose one of the worst results of slavery.

"The servants had to be sold to divide the estate. So Willis came to my father in great distress and fear of being separated from his family. My father could not stand by and see Willis' trouble. So 'Sis,' he said, 'You will have to wait for your piano. I cannot have Willis' wife separated from him,' and he bought Willis' wife and three children for him. He arranged for Willis and his family to move into a little plastered house on the edge of town. There Willis proceeded to pick up odd jobs to support them. But he had as little idea of making a living for them as his Master had of making money out of them, so it ended in my mother having a rather poor cook in the kitchen, who used the turpentine bottle instead of the essence of lemon, and spoiled the pies, first thing."

During this time, it was almost unheard of for a prominent family like the Porters to break the state laws against teaching slaves how to read, but Porter's daughter did so with obvious parental approval and support.

Brent recalled, "Willis Hodges was my first pupil. He developed an ambition to read, so every night in the kitchen, he could be seen bending over the book with his Master's little daughter guiding him along in the spelling book. The money he earned as a laborer in the Navy Yard came back, much of it, into his own pocket, and many nights I came up from his lessons with my pocket full of peanuts, or with a little peach turnover from those Matilda had made for him to sell to the workmen in the Navy Yard the next day. It was a rather unusual state of affairs and one that Northern people would find it hard to understand."

Just a few months later, the cities of Portsmouth and Norfolk were hit by a natural disaster of national proportion that would have a profound effect upon the Porters and their fellow citizens.

Once again the Porters and the Hodgeses were to be brought together, this time in the life and death struggle of an epidemic. But before that, Porter was given his first major conversion project when he was ordered to save a national treasure—the 1812-era frigate USS *Constellation*.

CHAPTER THREE

Saving a Wooden Hull Treasure
Rebuilding the USS Constellation

When Porter returned to Portsmouth, he found a much-improved Gosport shipyard capable of overhauling and building the Navy's largest warships like the USS *Mississippi* and USS *Powhatan*. But just as important to Porter was his supervisor, Samuel Hartt, who had been the yard's chief naval constructor since July 1847. Hartt was only too happy to welcome a talented assistant like Porter as the yard's master shipbuilder. Under Hartt's direction, Porter would polish his talents and finally emerge as one of the nation's youngest and most able naval constructors.

The *Daily Southern Argus* for November 30, 1854, gives a detailed picture of the projects then underway at Gosport. "The Gosport Navy Yard presents a busy aspect. Over 1400 workmen being industriously and cheerfully employed. The work in progress consists of the following items:

> Building the two new steamers, *Colorado* and *Roanoke*
> Fitting out the *Raritan, Potomac* and *Constellation*
> Building No. 14, a large, handsome, new Navy Store House.
> Completing an extensive saw shed.
> Completing the very lofty and long ship shed over ship 48.
> Getting in preparation the building of an extensive foundry.
> Repairing and improving the officers' elegant premises.
> Building the new Quarry Wall.

15

"Besides numerous other small works necessary to completely equip and furnish it as the first Navy Yard in the Union.

"The Navy Yard covers about a hundred acres. Commodore Breese and Captain Barron seem to be impressed with the importance of the large public interests entrusted to them, and attend sedulously and pleasantly to their duties, and encourage the good feeling that exists between them and the various departments; while the rest are imbued with a proper regard for the various duties belonging to them respectively."

On July 4, 1853, Samuel Hartt announced to Porter and his staff of shipwrights that he had just received an appointment as the Navy's Chief of the Bureau of Construction, Equipment and Repairs, which of course meant a major promotion. Hartt's new position, however, required him to visit Washington and other shipyards to supervise new projects. Meanwhile, Porter, age 40, would serve in Hartt's absence as Gosport's acting Naval Constructor. As fate would have it, on Porter's shoulders rested the awesome task of salvaging what could be saved of the famous 1797 Baltimore-built frigate USS *Constellation* that won so much fame with her sister frigate USS *Constitution* during the War of 1812. However, the news that Porter first received from the shipyard's timber inspector, John Jarvis, was not promising. *Constellation* was destined for "Rotten Row." According to Jarvis, if there were any further delays, little, if anything, of the ship could be saved. Meanwhile, the proposal that she be equipped with a new steam auxiliary system and propeller was denied, less she lose what character and personality she had left as a historic sailing warship. During his first inspection, Porter knew there was no escaping the fact that the vast majority of her main timbers were either rotted or unfit for further service. In Porter's mind, the entire integrity of the frigate was in question.

To preserve what he could of her original wooden frame and still produce a fighting frigate that bore the name and some resemblance to the original *Constellation*, Porter labored over her original plans drawn by venerable ship constructors Joshua Humphreys and Josiah Fox. Acting on his orders to save the historic vessel and yet bring her up to modern specifications as an active fighting ship, Porter decided to make some radical changes in her original configuration. Just how much timber

Porter replaced and what internal and external modifications he made has been the subject of much conjecture and controversy ever since. This much is known definitely.

On February 25, 1853, with the band from the USS *Pennsylvania* playing patriotic music that would traditionally be heard at a launch, *Constellation* was hauled into one of the shipyard's slips. The *Beacon* announced that she was "to be razed and converted into a first-class sloop-of-war, and will be otherwise throughout and extensively repaired."

Porter did not waste time once the ship was secured in position. Throughout 1853, he directed the tearing away of her extensive outer layers and bottom timbers. At first progress was tiring and tedious, but slowly, Gosport shipwrights began to take her apart plank-by-plank and rib-by-rib. The *Daily Southern Argus* on Monday, July 11, 1853, described the scene. "This old time-honored and time-worn frigate of historical memory has been literally torn to pieces preparatory to the building of the new *Constellation.* Hundreds of men are employed, directly or indirectly, upon her massive keel, which has been placed in one of the ship houses. She will be finished with all possible dispatch. . . . Her timbers are to be of live oak, every piece of which will be inspected by Mr. Jarvis."

By August 2, 1854, the *Argus* was able to describe in detail how much the original *Constellation* had been changed under Porter's direction.

"This vessel, now ready for launching at the Gosport Navy Yard, presents to the eye a structure of strength and capacity scarcely equaled in our Navy, . . . a first-class frigate. Below, we give her dimensions and armaments:

	Feet	Inches
Length of the load water line	176	05
" spar deck	182	00
" over-all	201	06
" Depth of spar deck	28	00
" Beam, extreme	42	02
Height between gun deck and spar deck	6	00
" " berth and gun decks	5	09
Tonnage........1400 "		

Finally, the day of reckoning had come. Porter stood dripping with perspiration along with a crowd of thousands on Saturday, August 26, 1854, as riggers prepared the rebuilt USS *Constellation* for launch. At first there was a loud cheer from those on the riverbank, then silence as she slid into the river at exactly twenty minutes before noon from her massive ship house. As the venerable warship passed down the ways, a web of mooring lines brought her safely to a halt.

A loud cheer went up and carried across the river from a sea of pleasure craft carrying hundreds of onlookers along the shipyard. Then the opposite shore of the Elizabeth replied with a final cheer. The *Constellation* would now sail again thanks to the talented craftsmen of Gosport and her newly improved design by Porter. Although the reconstruction of the *Constellation* was done under Porter's supervision, he would always share the credit with his senior mentor Samuel Hartt.

Because of Porter's highly successful conversion, the "new" *Constellation* had a challenging career ahead of her in anti-slavery patrols off Africa as flagship of the African Squadron. From April 1862 through May 1864 she served as a picket vessel in the Mediterranean and later off Cuba protecting U.S. shipping against Confederate sea raiders. From 1865 until 1933, she continued to build upon her famous legacy while serving as both a receiving ship and training vessel at Norfolk, Philadelphia, Pennsylvania, Annapolis, Maryland, and finally Newport, Rhode Island. After several emergency relief cruises and commemorative voyages, a group of concerned citizens from Baltimore adopted her for restoration and preservation after she was stricken from the Navy's active ship list in 1955. As a final testimony to Porter's talents, she remains moored as a very popular museum ship on the Baltimore waterfront.

However, those festive moments surrounding the launch of *Constellation* were soon lost just a few months later. Both Portsmouth and Norfolk were devastated by a yellow fever epidemic.

CHAPTER FOUR

Yellow Fever Epidemic

In 1855, the merchant ship *Ben Franklin* was placed in quarantine in Norfolk Harbor just down from Gosport. The vessel had arrived from the West Indies where an outbreak of yellow fever had ravaged the population. Breaking quarantine restrictions set by the Norfolk harbor master, and without notifying any Portsmouth officials, she arrived at Gosport's Page and Allen shipyard. Once again breaking the rules of quarantine and alerting no one, members of her crew opened hatches and pumped her bilge into the Elizabeth River. In a matter of weeks, a swarm of mosquitoes, released from the *Ben Franklin,* spread across Hampton Roads, decimating the citizens of both Norfolk and Portsmouth with yellow fever.

To protect his family, Porter evacuated them to Washington, DC. Returning to an empty house, he joined in the relief effort, turning his home into a refuge for the poor. According to his daughter, there was little medical comfort to offer those who were stricken as she reflected upon the first days of the epidemic before her evacuation.

Brent wrote, "I remember very clearly peeping through the slats of the closed front windows at the procession of people, ill of the disease, carried by, in carts, on their way to the pest houses, built just out of town, for the hope of the authorities at first was to segregate the patients. Hundreds died of it. Everybody went away who could get away. All business stopped; people were fed by contributions sent by neighboring cities and towns.

"A citizens' relief board was formed to look after the poor and sick and bury the dead, and at one time people died so fast they could not make coffins enough for them. They were buried in boxes of any sort which could be found."

According to Brent, the cure was basic and often not successful. "A patient was put into a hot mustard bath, in a bath tub, then taken out and wrapped in blankets. If this broke the fever, the patient recovered; if not, there was no other remedy, he died, and with little delay."

During the Yellow Fever Epidemic, Porter cared for his slave family as well. "My father," remembered Brent, "brought all of them home, found a used bath tub and patched it up and made arrangements to take care of them. He had so much trouble getting Willis Hodges to come that he left him alone in the little whitewashed house on the edge of town.

"Then Willis was taken with the fever, and no conveyance could be found to bring him home to the necessary bath tub. Finally my father thought of a wheelbarrow; so he had two negro women lift Willis into a wheelbarrow and roll him home. Willis did not die; he got well, and when, shortly afterwards, my father himself was taken with the fever, the black man showed what he was made of. For three days and nights he stayed by his Master, never changing his clothes, never neglecting him one minute in his helplessness, with all his people away, until the fever broke and the danger was past, and a day afterwards the Washington paper contained an item that Mr. John L. Porter was recovering nicely from a light attack of yellow fever." Finally after the first frost of winter, Porter was able to return to Washington and retrieve his family, who welcomed him with his last child, James. Once the family was resettled in Portsmouth, another historic opportunity awaited him at Gosport.

CHAPTER FIVE

Politics, Prayers and Steam Frigates

Porter spent the remainder of 1856 at Gosport shipyard building one of six new warships the Navy had ordered in response to a naval arms race that had precipitated in Europe from the Crimean War. Although the British and French had decided to develop steam driven ironclads, the United States Navy chose the more cautious course of building six wooden-hull steam "auxiliary" frigates. Equipped with steam engines and single propellers for auxiliary use only, the steam frigates would depend upon sails at sea and only utilize their engines when navigating a harbor. Apparently Porter's 1846 ironclad model had been pushed further back by "old navy" enthusiasts determined to preserve the age of wooden hulls driven only by the wind in canvas sail.

Brent described the notoriety her father received for this project.

"That winter my father was building a warship the *Colorado* for the Government over in the Navy Yard, and Mr. Hartt was building another alongside of it, the *Columbia*. The ships were launched in the early spring of 1856, a wonderful sight for one little girl, and the two builders received their commissions as Full Constructors in the Navy at that time."

It was indeed fortunate for Porter to have built a steam frigate so close to the Civil War. His familiarity with the lines and internal arrangements of *Colorado*, a sister ship of the steam frigate USS *Merrimac(k)*, would give him a distinct advantage when he began *Merrimac(k)*'s conversion into the ironclad CSS *Virginia*.

Giving Porter even more insight into the steam frigates was the simultaneous construction of the steam frigate *Roanoke* at Gosport.

Even though they were already obsolete when compared to Britain's ironclad HMS *Warrior* and France's ironclad *La Gloire*, by the time they were launched, the American steam frigates were nonetheless awesome warships that would achieve their own measure of glory during the Civil War. Porter's *Colorado* plan revealed a heavily armed, three-masted frigate nearly 264 feet long, with a 52 feet, 6 inch beam, that required a draft of 22 feet. The gundeck carried quite a punch with 2 10-inch guns, 28 9-inch guns and 14 8-inch guns. The steam frigate required a crew of 646 men and officers. However, the whole series of steam frigates held a special place in naval history for their engine problems. They burned an inordinate amount of coal when their sails were furled during harbor transits. Because of their heavy armament and munitions, in addition to their large coalbunkers, they were given to roll badly in normal seas. Their deep drafts, which required 22-feet of water for safe passage, severely restricted their operational capacity to deep water only. However, when raw firepower was considered, they were formidable.

Later Porter would reflect on how difficult it would be to break the blockade with ships like the *Colorado* positioned around the coastline of the Confederacy. In fact *Colorado* led the way in intercepting southern ships and harassing southern ports at will, inflicting early damage on Confederate positions at Pensacola, Florida, and later during amphibious operations around Fort Fisher, North Carolina. Following a series of diplomatic cruises to Asia, she engaged Korean forces after being fired upon in 1871. For a ship design that was touted to be a throw back to the past, the steam frigate *Colorado* had her share of the action until she was decommissioned and sold in 1885. Porter was justifiably proud when *Colorado* earned some of the glory of "Old Ironsides" after she withstood six direct hits from Confederate batteries during operations off Fort Fisher with the loss of only one man, and continued to hold her position and return fire.

Meanwhile *Roanoke, Colorado*'s sister ship built at Gosport, scored a number of early victories in the Civil War when she destroyed the schooner *Mary* off Lockwood's Inlet, NC, on 13

July 1861. She also took part in the capture of the Confederate schooners *Albion* and *Alert* and the ship *Thomas Watson* off Charleston, South Carolina, on 15 October 1861. She was frustrated, however, during the first day of the Battle of Hampton Roads as her draft prevented her from coming to the aid of USS *Cumberland* and *Congress* when her former sister, USS *Merrimac(k)*, now ironclad CSS *Virginia,* destroyed both on 8 March 1862. She was, however, able to contribute some aid to the crews of both *Cumberland* and *Congress* when she embarked 268 men from both wrecks and transported them safely to New York. Ironically, like her sister *Merrimac(k)*, she also took on a new identity during the Civil War.

Once she arrived in New York, *Roanoke* was taken to the construction site of the USS *Monitor* at Greenpoint, New York, and transformed into a three-turreted ironclad warship. At first it was hoped that she would become the U.S. Navy's first seagoing ironclad, but due to structural weaknesses, she was forced to remain a harbor defense vessel in Hampton Roads until the end of the war.

It was during the middle 1850's, when Porter's family interest in politics came to the forefront. As Brent wrote, Porter had more than a passing note in politics that would interrupt the peace and calm of their household.

"That year, 1856, marked the election of James Buchanan for President and John C. Breckenridge for "Vice", Brent recalled, "and gave me my first idea of politics." "My father was a Democrat, my Uncle Joe a Whig. There was some excitement, but not to be mentioned in comparison with the storm (Civil War) that broke four years later. The Democrats in Portsmouth celebrated their victory with a torch-light parade. All the Democrats illuminated their houses, and the processions marched all over town and whooped and yelled as they passed each illuminated house. My father's porch was draped in United States Flags, with a lighted lantern hung from the ceiling, and across the house in large letters made of barrel staves were the letters "Buck and Breck" (Buchanan and Breckinridge). But in the Porter home, Methodism always remained a central theme.

"One of my greatest pleasures was the Sunday afternoon walks with my father," recalled Buxton. "First, after dinner came the old fashioned Methodist bible class meeting. The religion of my people meant everything to them. There was no trifling about it.

"My father was the class-leader and they met at our house. First they sung a hymn, then prayed, then my father talked a little on some point of experimental religion. Then he proceeded to question each one on his or her spiritual condition and their state of minds and good consciences. Each one spoke out, almost like a Catholic confessing to a priest, owned their failures and hoped to do better. Then came a few words of admonition or encouragement from the leader, a verse sung or a hymn, and the next was called on by the leader as to what God was doing for her soul, and there was no doubt in the hearts of those people that God was dealing with their souls.

"Then came the walk with my father, with my little brother Jim in his carriage. My dear father took us over to the Hospital Park, through the Hart Woods, around the shore, when he would wait for me to make sand houses and play. Sometimes we went over to Swimming Point bridge and got to the water that way; then again around by the wharves where the shipping lay, but always we walked somewhere near water."

There is something so revealing in those last words of the above sentence. Brent's quote, "But always we walked somewhere near the water," explains Porter's character perhaps better than any single phrase. Both nautical-minded and spiritually-guided by its connotation, Porter's daughter had seen the entire man, both internal and external, and what drove him. She captured the character of the man remarkably well in so few words.

CHAPTER SIX

On the Brink at Pensacola

At the end of 1856, the tranquil life style of the Porters was interrupted again when he was ordered to Pensacola Navy Yard, Pensacola, Florida. Obviously Porter was excited about the new assignment and left several months ahead of his family to get established and find a suitable home for them and the family of slaves Willis and Matilda Hodges. During the fall of 1857, he returned home to take his family to Florida. His son George, who had been his apprentice in Gosport, was appointed as his father's clerk and draftsman. (This became their work arrangement for the duration of the war.) After a long train ride that took them to the steamer landing at Montgomery, Alabama, the Porters boarded the steamer *Le Grand* for a trip down the Mississippi to Mobile, Alabama.

"At Mobile, two ways were open to take us to Warrington, the village where the Navy Yard was built, nine miles south of Pensacola," wrote Brent. "One by stage, an all night trip, much crowded and fatiguing; the other by water on the Gulf of Mexico, which was generally a few hours trip by daylight. So my father decided on trying the schooner *Rebecca,* Captain Jones, which was at the wharf and which made regular trips from Mobile to Warrington. It proved an unfortunate decision.

"The wind had died down after a storm on the Gulf the day before, but had left the rolling, tossing billows. Everybody was seasick and the little schooner, not over clean, with a skipper not immaculate looking, stayed on the Gulf all day, all night, and we occupied the cabin of the Captain and the crew, to the supreme disgust of my fastidious mother and sisters. There was no telling how long we would stay there, until a breeze came up. I was frightened, and, as I had learned to do even that early in life, I got off into a corner and prayed for help. Well, we made some progress, and finally came into full view of the mouth of Pensacola Bay, and then, Oh! Blessed sight! Came something, long and black, out of the bay which, to the spyglass in my father's hands, revealed a big row-boat, manned with sailors, with brother George sitting in the stern. He had learned we were on the *Rebecca*, and seeing from the signal flag that a schooner was out there, he got the boat from the Commodore and the sailors rowed out into the Gulf to us, and our troubles were over. We were soon in our new home and a nice comfortable home it was.

"The Pensacola Navy Yard was quite pretty, well laid out, with the spaces filled with great live oak trees. The row of officer's houses, thirteen in number, was quite imposing, all built of brick, and on the same plan, with two verandahs on all sides, above and below. The beautiful bay bounded it on the south and east, a high wall on the other two sides, with the villages, Warrington and Woolsey, outside the west and north gates. Outside the northwest gate was the Methodist Church, devoid of paint, bare of every comfort and attraction. Thither on Sunday mornings we marched in a body.

"Papa was immediately elected Superintendent of the Sunday School. Mama and my sisters taught classes and brother John took charge of the empty book case and proceeded to print cards, soliciting subscriptions to the library, and to send all the scholars out begging. The books were bought, though I think my father contributed the lion's share of the collection and brother John was installed as librarian. Twice a month a minister came and held morning service. On the other two Sundays we attended the Chapel inside the Navy Yard."

In the summer of 1858, Porter's oldest son George left for Portsmouth where he was married in June 1859. He would remain in Portsmouth until the Civil War when he would rejoin his father in the Gosport constructor's office as an assistant draftsman. Porter's younger son John returned to Portsmouth as well to begin studies at the Virginia Collegiate Institute with the youngest,

Martha Buxton Porter (Brent), following him to the same school. Porter's other daughter, Alice, left Pensacola for studies at the Methodist College at Murfreesboro, North Carolina. Mary Susan, the second oldest, married the family minister in Pensacola, the Reverend John S. Moore. Porter would later write a now famous letter to Moore during the Civil War that contained a contemporary drawing of the CSS *Virginia* while still under conversion at Gosport. The letter is now preserved in the Museum of the Confederacy in Richmond, Virginia.

Meanwhile Porter supervised the construction of the screw sloop of war USS *Seminole*, a ship that would play a significant role in his life later in the Civil War.

Seminole's design required an overall length of 188 feet, with a beam of 30 feet, six inches, to support her 801 tons. She carried a crew of 120 sailors and one 11-inch Dahlgren smoothbore, one 30-pound Parrott rifle, and one light 12-pounder.

By 25 June 1859, *Seminole* was ready to be launched, and the honor fell to Porter's daughter, Martha Buxton Porter (Brent) to help christen the ship. Brent later entered the following notes in her memoir, which again revealed her father's character and his caring for the shipyard workers, both white and black.

"Then came the greatest happening of my life, I helped christen a ship! My father finished the *Seminole*, and by the Commodore's invitation, (and his daughter's willingness), the honor came to me to assist.

"So, dressed in my very best, fine deep embroideries and blue ribbons, escorted by an officer in full dress, I walked on board the ship, he carrying the bottle of claret with a loop for my wrist, which my father had made ready, to be broken over the bow as it touched the water and named *Seminole*.

"I think I was a dignified little girl for with the number of officers around joking and teasing, I remember perfectly that I behaved. The sponsor was launched on the ship in those days, not standing on the platform alongside as now. The time was in getting off. The ship with no engines and no ballast stood high out of the water, but rafts were brought alongside and a long rope ladder swung up and, with an officer going down without a tremor, and took my seat between them in the waiting rowboat to be pulled ashore by sailors.

"My father held a reception of gentlemen afterwards and by his invitation the gang of colored men who had worked on the ship came too. They were met at the porch by my father with a little speech and a goodly bank bill handed to their leader to treat the crowd. My father was a total abstinence man, but I am very sure he knew what was bought with his present and that many a lip was smacked over it." No one could have known at the celebration that in less than two years, *Seminole* would be assigned to capture or destroy the CSS *Virginia*.

Commissioned on April 25, 1860, *Seminole* sailed three months later for Brazil and remained on station until the outbreak of the Civil War. Ironically her first assignment was to serve on blockade duty off Hampton Roads in an effort to prevent supplies from reaching her former builder, John L. Porter and Gosport shipyard. After capturing the Confederate prize schooner *Albion* off Charleston, SC, she returned to Hampton Roads, anchoring off Newport News, 19 August, for recoaling. She later engaged the rebel armed tug *Harmony*, however, her target steamed out of range. After returning to action off South Carolina during which she participated in the capture of Port Royal and the bombardments of Forts Walker and Beauregard, she returned to Hampton Roads on March 25, 1862. This time her objective was to strengthen a fleet of ships assigned to keep the ironclad CSS *Virginia* from inflicting any further damage. One wonders what Porter must have thought when he heard that his former *Seminole* had arrived on the scene. A possible battle between *Seminole* and *Virginia* must have cost him some anxious moments.

Fortunately for both sides, that battle was never to take place. Prior to a Federal amphibious landing at Ocean View to recapture Norfolk and Portsmouth in the Spring of 1862, *Seminole* traded fire with rebel batteries at Sewell's Point on 8 May 1862. Following the Confederate withdrawal from Hampton Roads, she was ordered to New York Navy Yard for repairs.

Seminole was recommissoned on 8 June 1863 and sailed to the West Gulf Blockading Squadron. On the way she to the West Gulf Blockading Squadron. On the way she captured the Confederate steamer *Charleston* on 11 July. Two months later she captured the British steamer *Sir William Peel* with a cargo of 1,000 bales of cotton. On August 5, 1864, *Seminole* participated in the Battle of Mobile Bay. Lashed alongside USS *Lackawana*, she passed Confederate batteries at the bay's entrance, but then cast off on her own once the action became general. After the CSS *Tennessee* surrendered, rebel prisoners were taken aboard *Seminole*. During subsequent actions, Federal ships, including *Seminole,* cleared enemy torpedoes and bombarded Fort Morgan until it surrendered on 23 August. Badly in need of repairs, she pulled off station for Pensacola, Florida where she remained until 14 September. Assigned to patrol duty off Galveston, Texas, she remained in active duty off the Texas coast and finished the war with a flourish, capturing the schooner *Josephine* on 14 January 1865. During her last action of the war, she landed forces on the Confederate blockade-runner *Denbigh* on 23 May and helped burn her. Decommissioned at Boston on 11 August and subsequently laid up, *Seminole* was sold on 20 July 1870.

While at Pensacola, Porter was recognized, not only as a talented naval constructor during the building of *Seminole*, but also as a compassionate man who genuinely cared about the welfare of his workers. From his apprenticeship in Portsmouth onward, he was an ardent supporter and participant in daily shipyard prayer meetings and bible readings usually held before work or during lunch time. According to family history, this was a tradition he faithfully carried on throughout his career, including the Civil War.

When shipyard workmen asked him to intervene on their behalf, he did not hesitate to plead their cases to military superiors. A good example of his interest in the welfare of shipyard workers occurred while he was naval constructor at Pensacola in the winter of 1861.

The Navy Department had cut off the yard workers' wages since 1 November 1860, forcing Pensacola shipyard commandant James Armstrong to write a very curt letter to Secretary of Navy Isaac Toucey on January 8, 1861, demanding that wages be reinstated and past wages paid. Porter permitted one of his to the shipyard's executive officer, Captain E. Farrand.

Porter also took direct action in the matter of back wages owed the workers. He signed a resolution from the shipyard's civilian leaders demanding that Armstrong, "authorize an issue of provisions from the navy store to those who are in want, such issue to be deducted from the amounts due them respectively on the navy yard pay rolls for the months of November and December, 1860." To help relieve the situation, Porter asked to call on Armstrong on the morning of 9 January to represent the grievances of his department. On January 10th, Secretary Toucey agreed with Armstrong and Porter's demand that the ship's store be used to offset the owed wages. But this gesture of benevolence was hardly enough to prevent a growing rift between a majority of southern workers and their U.S. Navy leaders. Once the tocsins of secession began to sound, the subject of back wages would take a minor place against the backdrop of war. Porter would be in the middle of arbitration once more, but as he was later to testify before a U.S. Navy Court of Inquiry, the shipyard management was not in touch with events in the surrounding community nor were they prepared to deal with the gravity of the situation once a clear and present danger presented itself.

CHAPTER SEVEN

In the Middle of a Civil War

From the beginning of hostilities in 1861, Porter was against secession and felt the United States Navy should have fortified and held its southern shipyards. He felt that the seizure of federal property by his fellow southerners was a disgrace. In his notebook, he described his dissatisfaction regarding the loss of Pensacola on January 12, 1861, to a combined force of Florida and Alabama militiamen.

"During the Presidential Canvass for 1860, I was stationed as Naval Constructor in the Naval Yard at Pensacola, Florida. As soon as it was known that Lincoln was elected, the Secessionists began their work of breaking up the Union. They declared they would not live under a government that would not allow them to carry their slaves into any of the U.S. Territories and protect them."

The fact that Commodore Armstrong surrendered the Pensacola Navy Yard and was subsequently court-martialed and suspended for five years from active service was duly noted. "A Convention of the State (Florida) was soon called and a majority elected who soon passed the Ordnance of Secession. A battalion of volunteers, consisting of five companies, came from the interior of Alabama, surrounded the Yard immediately after the Ordinance was passed. Commodore Armstrong surrendered the Yard to them (A combined force of Escambia County, Florida militiamen were augmented by those from Montgomery County, Alabama) without having fired a shot. He was court-martialed for his deed and suspended for five years."

According to the *Official Records*, on February 8, 1861, a naval court of inquiry was convened in Washington, DC to consider the charges of dereliction of duty against Commodore James Armstrong and whether to pursue a court-martial against him. Porter, meanwhile, had been reassigned to the Washington Naval Yard several days after the surrender. While on station in Washington, he was busy fitting out the USS *Pawnee*. While directing the installation of machinery in the newly built USS *Pensacola*, which he designed back in Pensacola, he was called by the Navy's Judge-Advocate to give testimony about the loss of Pensacola. Again Porter voiced anti-secessionist sentiments during the interrogation.

After Porter was sworn in, the Judge Advocate began a question and answer segment, which is presented here from the *Official Records*.

"*Question.* What is your position in the Navy and were you present on duty at the U.S. navy yard near Pensacola, Fla. on the 12th of January?

Answer. I am (a) naval constructor. I was present on duty at the yard at that time.

Question. State as briefly as you can such material facts connected with the surrender of the yard as came under your observation.

Answer. On the morning of the 12th, Saturday, a couple of workmen, ship carpenters, came to my house early, about sunrise, and stated that a force had come to take the yard. I came out as soon as I had had my breakfast and heard in the yard that the force was then on its way to take the yard. The men I spoke of came from Warrington (in 1861, a growing village of shipyard families adjacent to Pensacola) and had heard there of the arrival of troops and that they were coming down to take the commodore prisoner (Commodore James Armstrong, commandant of the Naval Yard, Pensacola and commanding officer, Pensacola, Naval Station). At 1 o'clock I was at the muster office, and when the roll was called but few of the workmen answered. I heard the troops had arrived. I went up the yard and saw the officers ride in; Commander Farrand (Captain Ebenezer Farrand, executive officer, Pensacola Naval Station) conducted them in; they went to the commodore's office. I went to see the troops, and when I came back the flag had been hauled down. The troops then marched in and went to the marine barracks and the barracks at Fort Barrancas. I heard no conversation that passed between the commissioners and Captain Armstrong relative to the surrender.

Question. What was the strength of the force brought against the yard?

Answer. About 350 men. I noticed them particularly-I mean the column that halted in front of the yard. I do not know how many went to the magazine. I do not know of my own knowledge that any went there. I counted the companies and averaged the men. There were seven companies, and averaged about 50 men each-two from Montgomery, Ala., two from Wetumpka, Ala., and one from Lowndes, Ala., and two from Pensacola, Fla. All were uniformed companies except one from Pensacola; that was a new company. One of the Pensacola companies was part mounted and part on foot, and had double-barreled guns. The rest of the companies were well armed with rifled muskets and revolvers; they had no artillery. On Sunday a large uniformed company of 60 men came from Alabama, and on Wednesday following 350 more troops arrived by the *Oregon,* mostly from Mississippi, and on Thursday the steamer *Oregon* brought over from Mobile 300 or 400 more men; so that by that night they had 1,000. The steamer passed between the forts and the yard.

Question. What number of men were there in ordinary at the yard at the time of surrender, or had been there shortly before the surrender?

Answer. I should judge that there were sixty men in ordinary at the yard before the surrender. Before its surrender thirty of them had been sent to the fort. They were sent about three days before the surrender. They were sent to aid in the transportation of stores and munitions of war from Fort Barrancas to Fort Pickens. They had a large coaling lighter with them belonging to the navy yard to carry the stores, and the *Wyandotte* towed them backward and forward.

Question. What knowledge have you of any disaffection in the command of Captain Armstrong?

Answer. As far as the military officers of the yard were concerned, I believe they were all loyal; but as regards the civil officers, the storekeeper, the master workmen, and all the clerks of the yard were strong secessionists. They used to say boldly in the yard that it would be taken possession of just as soon as Alabama and Florida went out of the Union. They, the master workmen, the clerks, and a few of the workmen, had joined an association pledged to sustain the Southern Confederacy when formed. The mechanics were generally strong Union men.

Question. What arrangements were made or directions given, to your knowledge, by Captain Armstrong for the defense of the yard, especially between the 9th and 12th of January?

Answer. Nothing that I know. I had an order from the commodore to hurry up the work on the *Wyandotte* and get her out of the dock as soon as possible. This was given on the Monday or Tuesday previous to the Saturday on which the yard was taken. The vessel was got out on Tuesday, took her powder on board Wednesday, and on Thursday she assisted in moving stores from Barrancas to Fort Pickens. *(Question by Captain Armstrong)*

Question. What was the condition of the population of Woolsey (shipyard village north of the Pensacola shipyard), Warrington shipyard village just west of the Pensacola shipyard), and Pensacola in reference to the attack on the yard? Did they or did they not sympathize with and countenance the movement?

Answer. I do not think they countenanced the movement, but they were awed and afraid to express their opinion. The workmen from the yard on the day of the election, prior to the arrival of the troops, all voted in a body against the secession candidates in spite of an appeal from Colonel Chase, whom they hooted; and they defeated those candidates in that county by the largest vote had at the yard. After secession they were intimidated by the leading secessionists, not by the military. They were afraid to oppose the movement. I do not think the commodore could have obtained the aid of a single workman to aid in the defense of the yard; not that they favored the movement, but that they were afraid to move against it.

Question. How long prior to the surrender was the election of which you speak?

Answer. About two weeks."

The preceding testimony was presented to Porter for his approval and placed in the official record of the court proceedings. Armstrong was subsequently court-martialed and suspended for five years from active service. Porter apparently had no objection to the verdict.

CHAPTER EIGHT

Home to Portsmouth

It was no doubt an anxious time for Porter during those momentous final days when the United States flag still flew over Pensacola. Sensing the growing crisis and realizing it was well known that he did not approve of secession, he applied for orders north to Gosport Navy Yard, Portsmouth, Virginia, to be with his family. One of his former instructors, Samuel Pook still held the position of naval constructor at Gosport, so Porter tried again to get a new assignment somewhere close to his family. Fortunately, shortly after rebel forces seized the yard, Porter heard some good news and jotted it down in his notebook. Ironically, he had not escaped a connection with "Pensacola" quite yet.

"Two or three days after the surrender, I received orders to report for duty at the Washington Naval Yard. The USS *Pensacola,* which I had lately built, was receiving her machinery. I was ordered to fit out the Steamer *Pawnee* and began work on her in March 1861." Less than one month later, he got his wish to return home to Portsmouth.

"Early in April, I learned that Samuel Pook, the Naval Constructor at Gosport Navy Yard (since May, 1859), was anxious to be transferred from that Yard. I applied to Mr. Welles (Gideon Welles), the Secretary of the Navy, and requested duty at Gosport. By the time Porter arrived in Portsmouth, the conditions that had driven him from Pensacola followed him to Gosport. On the day Virginia voted to secede, he made his decision.

"I reported to Commodore McCauley (Charles S., commander

of the Gosport shipyard since August, 1860) on the 17th day of April, 1861. Everything within the Yard was disorder and confusion. The workmen were standing around in groups about the Yard. No one was able to work."

Returning home after determining that war was inevitable, Porter talked quietly to family and friends about the future. At forty-eight years old, his career as a civilian naval constructor working for the United States Navy seemed guaranteed for success. He had spent his younger years building some of the great ships of the U.S. Navy during an important period of transition in naval design and construction from canvass sail to steam power and screw propellers. Although never known to have boasted in private or public about his considerable achievements as a naval constructor, he no doubt took quiet pride in the rebuilding of the famed wooden frigate USS *Constellation*, and the construction of the *Pensacola, Allegheny, Seminole* and the steam frigate *Colorado*. He must have also been fully aware that he was destined to one day hold the title of Chief Naval Constructor, United States Navy. He knew all too well that a decision to side with secession would throw all his earlier accomplishments and career plans aside forever. From a more pragmatic viewpoint, Porter was very familiar with the strengths of the North's maritime industries. His notebook carries a very candid analysis about the Confederacy's chances in war against the Union.

"I did not think from the beginning of the War that the Confederacy could succeed if the Federal Government chose to prosecute the War. It was a new government against an old one. We had a great many incompetent men placed in positions of trust and responsibility. We had no navy to keep our ports open, and no money but paper to carry on the War. We had no resources in men while the United States had all of Europe to draw from to fill up their decimated ranks. It was almost hoping against hope that we would ever gain our liberty."

Even though his strong opinion against secession had not changed since Pensacola, he now was forced to consider his family and their safety, the future of his community and Portsmouth and the Commonwealth of Virginia. Meanwhile he watched with disbelief as the commander of Gosport shipyard, Commodore Charles S. McCauley, began to lose control.

The April 20, 1861, destruction and evacuation of Gosport by the United States Navy forced Porter into making a decision. In his usual, matter-of-fact, way, Porter wrote, "I then resigned my appointment as Constructor in the U.S. Service and reported for duty to Commandant Forrest. The Commandant assumed command of the Yard for the State of Virginia."

CHAPTER NINE

The Stage Is Set
The Burning of Gosport

The conflagration of Gosport during the evening of 20 April 1861 must have horrified Porter and the entire population of Portsmouth and Norfolk. What he had feared would happen in Pensacola had now become reality in his hometown.

Porter described in his notebook what he saw that day. "At one o'clock the gates of the Yard were closed to the men and the destruction of the Yard began. U.S. Naval Officers and men began at once with the total destruction of the Yard. They sank the *Germantown* at the wharf, cutting down her masting, which fell across her, and made her a total wreck.

"They next went onboard the *Merrimac,* and broke all her small machinery, opened all her cockes, and sank her. The Sloop-of-War *Plymouth,* the *Columbus,* and *Delaware* were also sunk by them. They then commenced the destruction of the stores, small arms, etc. until nightfall. The *Pawnee* arrived that evening with Captain Paulding (Hiram Paulding). The vessel also carried a regiment of Massachusetts Volunteers. The regiment worked nearly all night firing the Yard and destroying property.

"By daylight, they had burned the *Germantown, Merrimac,* both of the shiphouses, the building near the gate, marine barracks, ships: *Porpoise, Pennsylvania, Brandywine, Potomac,* and all the vessels in ordinary. They then evacuated the Yard. The *Pawnee* towed the *Cumberland* toward Fort Monroe. It seemed that the old ship USS *United States,* was spared from destruction. (Later as CSS *Confederate States* she was sunk as an obstruction in the Elizabeth River.) The Confederates, upon their evacuation (May 1862), could not burn her either.

"Thus, in the short spree of four months, I had been attached to three Navy Yards, two of which had to be given up without any defense whatever. In my opinion, the Gosport Navy Yard could have been defended. It was disgraceful that Commodore McCauley was not called to account for his conduct like Commodore Armstrong of Pensacola."

William H. Peters, future Confederate Gosport shipyard paymaster and a close friend and neighbor of Porter also wrote an eyewitness account.

"At about 2 p.m. on April 20, Mr. William Spooner came to my place of business in Portsmouth and said the Navy yard gate had been closed and that none but those having special permits were allowed to enter the Yard. He also said it was rumored that the authorities of the yard were making preparations to destroy that establishment with fire.

"To satisfy ourselves as to the truth of these rumors, Mr. Spooner and myself procured a boat and sailed it up to and in front of the Yard as far as the timber dock."

What they saw must have first seemed unbelieveable. "All the ships alongside the wharves had been scuttled and were slowly sinking. Workmen were still busily engaged in cutting away the standing rigging of the sloop-of-war *Germantown*. Her masts were about to fall as other men broke off the trunnions of her guns." By the time Peters and Spooner returned, there was talk along High Street that the yard was about to be burned and that the fire might certainly engulf the entire city.

Porter joined other prominent men of the city who had been called to an emergency town meeting to find the best course of action to save Portsmouth and the shipyard. The group selected Samuel Watts and James Murdaugh, a relative of John Porter, and William H. Peters to negotiate with Captain McCauley before it was too late. The three were met at the yard gate by General Blow, Commander of the State Militia for the district, Lieutenant John Maury, and Paymaster John DeBree. Maury and Debree had just come from a meeting with McCauley during which they had tendered their resignations from the USS *Cumberland*. They

The Stage Is Set: The Burning of Gosport

informed the "Citizen's Committee" that McCauley would not see them and that they would not answer questions regarding the situation inside the brick wall boundary of Gosport. It was not too long before Watts, Murdaugh, and Peters made their way home before the night sky answered those questions about the future of the shipyard. Porter, waiting anxiously on his porch, could also see clearly that his worst fears were now realized. No doubt he must have wished that he had evacuated his family to Petersburg or Richmond.

Porter's son, J.W.H. Porter, an aspiring journalist and historian, who became a newspaper publisher after the war, took careful notes describing the events of April 20-21, 1861. His memoirs would be augmented after the war by the testimonies of fellow members of the "Stonewall Camp," Confederate Veterans, of Portsmouth, VA, and considerable discussions with his father. In 1892 the memoirs were published as a book entitled, *A Record of Events In Norfolk County, Virginia, From April 19th, 1861, To May 10th, 1862, With A History Of The Soldiers And Sailors Of Norfolk County, Norfolk City And Portsmouth Who Served In The Confederate States Army Or Navy* (Hereafter referred to as *Record of Events*).

"The Navy Yard was under the command of Commodore McCauley, who, under the very peculiar circumstances that surrounded him, was uncertain how to act, and the Navy Department at Washington left him without instructions. He had received orders on the 16th (April 1861) from the Department to immediately fit out the *Merrimac,* to put her guns on her without loss of time (they had been taken ashore), and to send her, with the other vessels capable of being moved, together with the ordnance, stores, etc., beyond the reach of seizure.

"Commodore McCauley construed the order to mean a desire on the part of the Navy Department to abandon the station, and did not feel authorized to the extent of bringing on hostilities by maintaining possession of the Navy Yard and firing upon the city of Portsmouth, more especially as the United States Government had made no hostile demonstration against the State of Virginia.

"There was at the Navy Yard at that time, the sloop-of-war *Cumberland,* 22 guns, in commission, with a full complement of officers and men on board; the sloops-of-war *Plymouth,* 22 guns, and *Germantown,* 22 guns, and the brig *Dolphin,* 6 guns, almost ready for sea; the steam frigate *Merrimac,* 40 guns, almost ready for sea and undergoing repairs; the line of battle ship *Pennsylvania,* 120 guns, in commission as a receiving ship, with a considerable crew on board, and the 74-gun ships *Delaware* and *Columbus,* and the frigates *Raritan, Columbia* and *United States,* dismantled and in ordinary. The force of sailors and marines on the various vessels and at the Navy Yard was probably about 600, well armed and abundantly supplied with ammunition. The *Plymouth, Germantown, Dolphin,* and *Merrimac* were lying alongside the wharves and men were working on them. The *Delaware* and *Columbus* were at a wharf at the southern end of the yard, and might have been considered as in 'Rotten Row,' a term applied to vessels for which the Government no longer had any use.

"Commodore McCauley might have held the Navy Yard for a considerable time against any forces at the disposal of the State of Virginia. The *Cumberland* and *Pennsylvania* could have swept it with their guns, and he has been considerably censured for not doing so, but there was another side to the question. The *Pennsylvania* might have been considered as stationary. She was supposed to have been fast in the mud, and could easily have been enfiladed by batteries on shore, in such a position that her broadside could not be brought to bear on them, and furthermore, it would have been possible, shut up in a close harbor as those two vessels were, to have captured them by a determined attack by boarders at night, just as General Magruder, later in the war, captured the steamer *Harriet Lane* in Galveston Harbor (Texas). By the erection of batteries on the St. Helena side of the river, opposite the Navy Yard, the *Cumberland* could have been driven away or destroyed. She would have been compelled to have relied upon her sails for motive power. It is true the State of Virginia had nothing heavier than twelve-pounder howitzers with which to man those batteries, but Commodore McCauley was not familiar with the resources of the State, and, therefore, in the light of the last orders he had received from Washington, determined to leave with what he could take with him and destroy the remainder. His determination was quickened by reports that reached him that the Virginia forces were sinking obstructions in the river below Fort Norfolk and erecting batteries. He was deceived also by the continued moving of trains on the Norfolk and Petersburg Railroad within hearing of the Navy Yard, and thought they were bringing troops to Norfolk. This was done by General Mahone, who was then president of the railroad company, for the purpose of creating just such an impression.

"The work of destruction began a little before noon on the 20th, and the frigate *Merrimac* was the first object of the destroyers. Carpenters and machinists were at work on her at the time. The carpenter of the *Cumberland,* with a small squad of sailors to assist him, opened her bilge cocks and she filled with water and settled quietly until she rested on the bottom. Owing to her great draft of water she did not settle far.

"After the 12 o'clock bell was rung for the watermen to knock off for dinner, the gates of the Navy Yard were closed, and no one was permitted to enter without the approval of the Commodore. The work of destruction then proceeded very rapidly. The standing rigging of the *Germantown* was cut away and the guys which held the heavy masting shears were cut in two, so that the shears fell across her and she was broke and sunk. The *Plymouth* and *Dolphin* also were scuttled, as were also the 74-gun ships *Delaware* and *Columbus,* but on account of their great depth they were not submerged.

"During the afternoon it became generally known in Portsmouth that the vessels and stores in the Navy Yard were being destroyed and a rumor became prevalent that it was the intention of Commodore McCauley to set the buildings on fire. This, it was feared, would cause serious damage in the city, as it was separated from the yard only by the width of Lincoln street, which was but sixty feet wide, and a meeting of citizens was held, at which Messrs. Samuel Watts, James Murdaugh and William H. Peters were appointed a committee to wait upon Commodore McCauley to endeavor to persuade him to reconsider that purpose, if he really entertained it, but the Commodore refused to see them and they were denied admission into the yard."

Now that the shipyard was all but destroyed, Porter's worry about the fate of his family and the city of Portsmouth must have increased dramatically as word quickly spread that just at dusk the screw sloop-of-war *Pawnee*, under Captain Hiram Paulding, had just steamed to Gosport as flames began to clearly light the adjacent waterfront. No doubt at this point Porter knew there would be war, and having just finished fitting out the *Pawnee* weeks earlier at the Washington Navy Yard, he had knowledge of what her eight nine-inch guns and two twelve-pounders could do. He most assuredly prayed throughout the evening that the *Pawnee* would not come steaming up the Elizabeth on the vanguard of a whole flotilla of Federal warships bombarding the city and nearby Norfolk at will. But that was not to be the case. Instead of firing on the city, Paulding had other orders. His men joined the wreckers already busy at work within the yard and then helped them carry out their order to burn the facility.

Pawnee had earlier stood helplessly off Fort Sumter on April 12, 1861, with other Federal warships while the garrison was steadily bombarded by shore batteries until the fort was surrendered the following day. Porter later learned with some degree of pride that she had successfully sailed up the Potomac on May 24, 1861, and played a major role in gaining Federal troops their first foothold in Virginia with the capture of Alexandria. But now she had taken on the role of the enemy.

J.W.H. Porter continued his report of the events he and his father witnessed during that momentous evening of April 20, 1861.

"The long building on the north front of the yard, facing Lincoln Street, and in which was the main entrance, was set on fire and totally destroyed. This building, among other things, contained the armory of the yard, and its hundreds of rifles, carbines, pistols, cutlasses, and other ordnance stores, besides ropes, canvas, etc. The two large ship houses, A and B, were also fired. Ship house A had in it, on the stocks, the 74-gun ship *New York*, completely framed, with her deck beams, carlines and knees completely, and partially planked, inside and out, and her decks partially laid.

"The fire from the ship houses communicated to the *Merrimac, Plymouth, Germantown* and *Dolphin,* and all of them that was above the water was consumed. The *Pennsylvania, Raritan* and *Columbia* were anchored out in the stream and shared the fate of the ship houses. They were set on fire and burned almost down to their keels. Several buildings, containing stores of various kinds, were fired and, together with their valuable contents, totally destroyed."

The Stage Is Set: The Burning of Gosport

In addition to a number of cannons being spiked, Drydock I, the nation's first granite drydock, was rigged to blow up, but the charge was discovered in time to prevent the explosion of some thirty barrels of gunpowder. Porter certainly had no way of knowing about the plot to destroy the drydock, but it was indeed a fortunate turn of events for him. It is highly unlikely that he would have found another facility in time to convert the burned hulk of the USS *Merrimac(k)* into CSS *Virginia*.

As the terrible night of 20 April continued until the early hours of April 21, winds swept flames from the burning ship houses to private homes along nearby Lincoln Street. Only a providential change in wind direction saved the rest of Portsmouth from being burned to the ground. Many citizens in Portsmouth, including Porter, probably thought that the *Pawnee* had begun shelling the city when the loaded guns of the burning *Pennsylvania* discharged from the heat.

Local rebels under Major General William B. Taliaferro took advantage of the confusion within the yard and what they perceived was the inability of Commodore McCauley to control events. Correctly guessing that he would accept any offer as he watched his command go up in smoke, Taliaferro proposed to McCauley that he would guarantee *Pawnee* and *Cumberland* safe passage if the shipyard was evacuated. In fact the rebels had no way to deal with either *Pawnee* or *Cumberland* at all, but given the circumstances within the Gosport walls, their ruse worked. About midnight, the *Pawnee* left the shipyard with the *Cumberland* in tow. As the American flag was lowered, Paulding sent word to the rebel forces that if any shots were fired at his men or those of McCauley, he would retaliate forcefully. The rebels correctly interpreted this to mean the shelling of Portsmouth and Norfolk and allowed the two ships to leave.

Before Porter retired for a fitful night of sleep, he learned that Norfolk County militiamen occupied the Norfolk County Court House and various points around the city. When he awoke at daybreak the following day, April 21st, he heard that rebel forces had marched into Gosport shipyard and that a close friend, Lieutenant C.F.M. Spotswood, had raised the flag of the Commonwealth of Virginia with Captain Robert B. Pegram in command. Porter knew instantly that his career as a naval constructor in the United States Navy was over and that now, even though it was against his better judgment, he must cast his lot with Virginia and the Confederate Navy. At the same time, his son, J.W.H. Porter, informed him that he had accepted a commission in the Confederate Signal Corps.

On April 22nd, Confederate Navy Captain French Forrest relieved Virginia Navy Captain Pegram as commanding officer of Gosport. Having resigned his commission as naval constructor that same day, Porter reported for duty to Captain Forrest as naval constructor, Virginia Navy. It was a decision that would take him from Gosport as naval constructor, 1861-1862, to Richmond, 1862-1864 and finally to Wilmington, North Carolina, 1864 to 1865. During that time he would rise to the top of his professional rank, being named by Secretary Mallory, Chief Naval Constructor, Confederate States Navy, 1 June 1864.

Like everyone around him, Porter was amazed at the amount of destruction within Gosport shipyard, but he was also relieved to hear what paymaster Peters listed in his inventory that survived. Peters's report made its way from the shipyard commander's office to Richmond, the new Confederate Capital, as public document No. 25 and listed the following as having survived the debacle of April 20-21, 1861: 1. The Commandant's dwelling, 2. The Commander's, Surgeon's, Lieutenant's, and Master's dwellings, 3. The foundry and its dependencies, 4. The machine shop and its adjuncts, 5. Five large storehouses of naval supplies, 6. Several workshops. The total amount of property completely intact, including Dry Dock I, timber dock, and the quay wharves, totaled $2,944,800.00. Giving the Confederates more advantage was the large amount of ordnance hastily abandoned by the Federals. Scattered about the yard in perfectly operable condition were a staggering 1,085 pieces of heavy cannon, with gun carriages, breechings, blocks and tackle; a large number of shells and stands of grapeshot; 250,000 pounds of powder, totaling $341,000.00. A massive amount of food provisions and clothing and small stores were left as well which totaled $38,763.00 and $56,269.00 respectively.

Porter's worry that the Confederacy was lacking an industrial base from which to build a new navy must have eased somewhat at this point. But he also knew there were many complex political hurdles in starting a new government. Having appeared before congressional hearings on naval matters before, he was all too familiar with his new leaders, Jefferson Davis, the new President of the Confederate States of America, and his Secretary of Navy, Stephen B. Mallory. In Porter's mind, there was no question which branch of government would be the most favored. Davis was an 1828 graduate of the U.S. Military Academy, West Point. He had served in action during the Mexican War where he had befriended Robert E. Lee. During the Franklin Pierce administration, he had served as Secretary of War and twice served as U.S. Senator from Mississippi.

Stephen B. Mallory, on the other hand, had risen through the ranks of Washington political seniority as U.S. Senator from Florida. Just before the Civil War, he was the Capital's most influential member on naval matters. Porter knew that Mallory was the type of politician who would at times favor his constituency over the welfare of the nation. However, as Chairman of the Naval Affairs Committee, Mallory had championed the idea of building an American ironclad as the British and French navies were doing with HMS *Warrior* and *La Gloire*. Ironically, it was also Mallory who fostered the career of Swedish inventor John Ericsson, who Porter would meet later, not in person, but in a contest of designs over drawing boards to build America's first ironclad.

With Virginia now firmly a member of the Confederacy and Gosport now under control of Confederate naval authorities by July 1861, Porter was forced to deal with the political leadership in Richmond. Once again, he had to face Mallory to advance his ideas about what immediate steps the Confederate navy should take against Abraham Lincoln's first strategy against the South— a blockade around her major ports. All that would have to wait for about a month while Confederate defenses in Hampton Roads and the Confederate army were strengthened with Gosport's arsenal.

Porter wrote, "In the beginning, most of the work being done was the moving of the guns, and the fitting-up of various batteries erected in the harbor and down the river to prevent the return of the Federals and clearing up the wrecks, all on the account of the State of Virginia, which had not yet joined the Montgomery

Government." (Montgomery, Alabama was the temporary seat of the Confederate government before it was moved to Richmond.) In the first of June 1861, he was joined by another family friend, William P. Williamson, the namesake of a famed naval physician who had served as Chief Physician at the United States Naval Hospital, Portsmouth, Virginia.

Williamson family papers state that William P. Williamson was born in Norfolk around 1810. His interests grew in a different direction from his father's medical profession as he evidenced early talents in mechanical engineering. While his father was stationed in New York, Williamson amazed his instructors with a precocious talent that was soon recognized by Navy officials once the family moved back to Portsmouth and took up residence at the Naval Hospital. He began an apprenticeship at Gosport Navy Yard that lead to employment at the yard's steam engineering division. At Gosport, Williamson soon became one of the foremost steam engineers in the country and pioneered early experiments in a variety of systems with Porter's close associate and friend, Lieutenant William W. Hunter.

By 1842, Williamson had been promoted at Gosport to supervisor of the yard's growing machine shop. He was subsequently promoted to Chief Engineer, U.S. Navy on October 10th of that same year. Porter's first major project with Williamson began during the construction of the steam frigate USS *Colorado*, which carried great portend of things to come. Less than two decades later, both would be peering into the burned hulk of *Colorado*'s sister ship, USS *Merrimac(k)*, at the almost identical auxiliary steam engines that would propel an entirely new type of warship. Like Porter, Williamson was not pro-secession or pro-slavery, but he held his loyalty to Portsmouth and his native state, Virginia, above all else. When shipyard commander Captain Charles McCauley asked Williamson to retake the oath of allegiance in 1861, he refused and was imprisoned. After his release, Williamson was dismissed from the U.S. Navy and joined the Confederate Navy on June 11, 1861, as Senior Engineer. By October 17, 1862, he was appointed Chief Engineer, Confederate States Navy.

The third member of Porter's team, and destined to be his permanent nemesis and enemy, was Lieutenant John M. Brooke.

The Stage Is Set: The Burning of Gosport

Born near Tampa, Florida on December 18, 1826, Brooke was a graduate of the U.S. Naval Academy. He resigned his commission on April 20, 1861, and accepted an appointment in the Confederate Navy with his former rank restored. Shortly after the Confederate government was moved from Montgomery to Richmond, Brooke was given responsibility for naval gun development and armor experiments. Early conversations between Brooke and Mallory in Richmond concerning the development of ironclad warships seemed to parallel the ideas of Porter.

Unfortunately an argument over rights to claim the invention of the CSS *Virginia* would cause a lifelong debate between the two, with Williamson taking the side of Porter since the constructor drew the *Virginia*'s plan from his earlier drawings made in 1846. (The author was extremely fortunate to study the plans during graduate work on a thesis about the conversion of the USS *Merrimack* into the CSS *Virginia* and believes they decide the argument in Porter's favor.)

But in the spring of 1861, Mallory needed all three to find some method to break the wooden hull blockade around the Confederacy's coastline. Now the work to build an ironclad began in earnest, and Porter was at the center of the project.

CHAPTER TEN

Ironclad Decision
Modification of the 1846 Plan

Realizing that the South was not prepared to meet the United States Navy in any contest, Porter knew it was time to present his plan for an ironclad drawn back in Pittsburgh in 1846. Unpacking his drawing tools that Spring of 1861 in the constructor's office adjacent to Gosport's Drydock I, he modified the original plan that Mallory's Navy Department would accept as the "prototype" from which to develop an ironclad navy.

In the beginning Porter knew that the South would try to defend its harbors and not be able to afford a large seagoing navy. Secondly, hard currency was too scarce. There was no time to waste limited resources building wooden frigates to match the Federal warships already in position off shore. Porter needed to provide Richmond with a vessel that could be built in months rather than years and inflict the heaviest damage possible on the wooden hull blockaders.

Using heavy paper that was measured in scrolls four-foot long and approximately 16 inches wide, he drew his plans and specifications. Acting upon his directions, several artisans followed his line drawings and turned the concept into a half-model from which he could make his presentation to Mallory and the shipyard commandant.

J.W.H. Porter wrote, "At that time Commodore Marshall Parks, President of the Albemarle and Chesapeake Canal Company, had been appointed by the State of North Carolina, to act in conjunction with Commander Muse, formerly of the United States Navy, as commissioner to purchase and fit out vessels for the North Carolina Navy, to protect the waters of the Albemarle and Pamlico Sounds, and, visiting the Gosport Navy Yard upon business connected with his (John L. Porter's) office, was shown this model by Mr. Porter, and was so impressed with it that he went to Raleigh, North Carolina and informed the Governor and members of the Legislature of the plan, and suggested that some small iron-clads be built for the defense of the North Carolina sounds. He was directed to prepare a "Bill" to authorize the Governor to have some vessels built on the plan, and it was passed immediately. The State of North Carolina, soon after this, decided to join the Confederacy, and Commodore Parks was directed to go Richmond and turn over all the steamers he had purchased and fitted out, to the Confederate States Navy Department, and therefore the iron-clads were not built."

Porter concentrated on adopting the original shield of his 1846 Pittsburgh plan, but while that vessel was designed for sea service as well as for harbor defense, his new model was designed only for harbor operations. At this point, he had not yet added the water break extending from the casemate to the bow.

According to J.W.H. Porter, who worked closely with his father and brother George on the adaptation of the 1846 model, "The vessel was designed to have been one hundred and fifty long on deck and one hundred and forty-four feet on the keel; forty feet beam at the knuckle and thirty-three feet across the bottom amidships. She was to have been built sharp at the bow and with flat bottom. Her draft of water was eleven feet, and she was fitted with a nine-foot propeller. Her knuckle was nine feet perpendicular from the bottom of her keel and her water line was two feet above her knuckle, so that the eaves of the vessel were submerged two feet below the water line. The shield covered the entire length of the vessel, was arranged at an angle of forty degrees, and was made circular at each end. The shield was to have had a thickness of wood and iron, or in other words, the eaves or knuckle of the ship, were to be two feet below the water line, just as he had planned in his Pittsburgh ship."

The original armament consisted of six 11-inch smooth bore guns, four broadside and one gun each at bow and stern. The

Ironclad Decision: Modification of the 1846 Plan

bow and stern guns were to be pivot guns and have a range out of three portholes. The broadside guns were on pivots also, and could fire out of each side. While the bow of the vessel was to be sharp, there was sufficient flare in her nine feet of depth from keel to knuckle, to take in the circular end of the shield. Porter's Pittsburgh model was built with sides inclined at an angle of forty-five degrees, but the angle of inclination of this vessel was forty degrees. He made this change because the ordnance in use in 1861 was heavier than that of 1846. Her deflection capabilities were in direct relation to her casemate's angle of resistance. With a good engine she would have made seven or eight knots.

Mallory was also in agreement that an ironclad navy was the right direction and brought this to the attention of the House Committee on Naval Affairs before they moved from Montgomery to Richmond. It was also no secret that both England and France were then experimenting on seagoing ironclads and Porter, although aware of how financially strapped the Confederate Navy was, made an early proposal to Mallory for the purchase of one or more seagoing vessels. According to J.W.H. Porter's *Record of Events*, his effort was ignored at the beginning of the war when it could have made a critical difference.

However, on the 22 of June 1861, Porter received orders to report to the Navy Department at Richmond. Although the orders did not detail the reasons for which he was to report, Porter took advantage of the opportunity to carry his now-finished model and modified plans of the Pittsburgh ironclad of 1846.

After his arrival in Richmond on June 23 (Sunday), 1861, he called at the Secretary's office the following day, and showed him the modified 1846 model and plan. Much to his satisfaction, Mallory immediately ordered a "Board" consisting of Porter, Chief Engineer William P. Williamson and Lieutenant John M. Brooke to review Porter's plan and model.

The Board met on 25 and 26 June, and, according to the statements of Messrs. Williamson and Porter, there was no other subject discussed except Porter's model and plan. Had Porter any worries that his concept would be subject to heavy criticism or doubt, they were soon put to rest as the board decided without reservation to recommend the building of an ironclad after Porter's modified version of his 1846 model. A general discussion followed the approval concerning the costs and schedules required to complete the project.

J.W.H. Porter gleaned from various memoirs the following dialogue from the meeting. Williamson remarked, "It will take at least twelve months to build her engines unless we utilize some of the machinery in the *Merrimac*." Porter answered, "Why can't you use it all? I can adapt this model to the *Merrimac* and utilize her machinery in her." Mr. Williamson replied, "I can."

It was therefore decided at once to recommend that the *Merrimac(k)* be converted into an ironclad. None of the board members appeared to have had any thought of using the USS *Merrimac(k)* previous to this meeting. Although Brooke would later argue that he first raised the idea of building an ironclad before Mallory at an earlier date. After the decision was made to utilize the burned hulk of the USS *Merrimac(k)*, the board met to consider Porter's 1846 modified model. Brooke supported Porter's claim before a Confederate Congressional investigating committee in February 1863. Brooke testified that, "The Secretary directed Constructor Porter, Chief Engineer Williamson and myself to meet him in my office here, and this model was examined by us all and the form of the shield adopted."

Porter and Williamson were the only members of the board who knew the condition of the *Merrimac(k)* and how much was truly left to salvage. No doubt they had several informal discussions about her engines as Porter felt confidant that he could build an iron casemated gundeck above them no matter what the condition of *Merrimac(k)*'s hull. Brooke would have had little involvement here since he had not seen the *Merrimac(k)* since the destruction of the Gosport Navy Yard when she was burned to the water's edge.

Meanwhile, Porter had already directed her salvage with the Baker Wrecking Company of Portsmouth, Virginia, on 30 May 1861. After ordering her placed in Gosport Shipyard's Drydock I, he made a thorough examination of the wreck and then asked Williamson to examine the machinery to determine if anything could be salvaged. After Williamson reported back to the constructor's office that indeed *Merrimac(k)*'s auxillary engines could be made to run, Porter immediately began further modifications to his original 1846 model to suit the burned hulk

Ironclad Decision: Modification of the 1846 Plan

if called upon to get something out quickly.

Mallory was convinced that Porter and Williamson could expedite the *Merrimac(k)'s* conversion. On 18 July 1861, he submitted a report to the Confederate Congress, in which he wrote: "The cost of this work is estimated by the constructor and engineer in charge at $172,523, and as time is of the first consequence in this enterprise, I have not hesitated to commence the work, and to ask Congress for the necessary appropriation."

Porter's plan, that called for the arrangement of an ironclad shield for glancing shots, mounting guns, arranging the hull and plating, was not submitted simultaneously with Mallory's congressional report since Porter was ordered to return to Gosport. Mallory determined it was critical that Porter begin the conversion of the *Merrimac(k)* by immediately surveying her machinery and making the necessary arrangements with Williamson to overhaul the engines. To begin his conversion plans, Porter took the first full and true measurements of the *Merrimac(k)*. The shipyard's senior carpenter James Meads assisted Porter with the measuring tape to complete the dimensions that were then transferred onto the conversion plan. During this work, Porter appointed Meads as Master Ship Carpenter.

With Porter looking on from his office window or standing at a makeshift table made from sawhorses and a flat board arranged at the drydock, Meads and his helpers cut away the burned section of the ship and built a wooden deck from one end to the other. Porter and Meads continually conferred with Master Blacksmith James Farmer during this work. In forming the shield, J.W.H. Porter observed that inside the shield the deck was covered with plank, on beams, but outside the shield, at both ends, it was built of solid timber, and covered over with iron one-inch thick.

The fire of April 20, 1861, had left the ship with only two decks, gun and berth decks and did little if any damage to the already submerged boilers and engines which Porter and Williamson left in their original positions. She was fitted with four-inch, hammered iron, port shutters on her four quarter ports, but even though it was planned, she had no shutters fixed to her other ports because of a shortage of time and iron. They were made in two pieces and closed like a pair of shears. She steamed from Gosport on March 8, 1862, before they were finished. In a

Record of Events, J.W.H. Porter noted that, "Her rudder chains were let into the outside after deck flush under the iron, and passed up through the shield in pipes until they came over the water line and were then conducted on rollers to the steering wheel."

Porter recorded the exact measurements of the *Merrimac(k)/Virginia* as "262 feet and 9 inches long from her stem to the after side of the stern post, and from the stem to the forward part of the shield was 29 feet 6 inches. From the tiller to the after part of the shield was 55 feet, and the length of the shield was 178 feet, 3 inches. The neat length on the gun deck, under the shield, was 167 feet, 7 inches." Meads's carpenters formed the rafters supporting the shield from yellow pine fourteen inches thick. They were then bolted together and fixed at an inclination of thirty-five degrees. A course of four-inch oak plank was added for further strength. All three of these courses of timber were caulked. The oak planks were plated over with a course of rolled iron bars, eight inches wide and two inches thick, running fore and aft. Porter then ordered another layer of similar iron run along the same course and then securely bolted from the outside of the shield through the iron and wooden and fastened on the inside of the shield with nuts. Porter later gave his son the following dimensions: "The length of the sides was twenty-four feet, and the perpendicular thickness was twenty-two inches of wood and four inches of iron, but horizontally, it was about four feet. The deck, or top of the shield, was fourteen feet wide and was protected by an iron grating made of two inch square iron with meshes two inches square. The pitch of the gun deck was seven feet. There were three hatchways in the top grating, with pivot shutters."

In the original drawings it was contemplated to build a pilot house at the forward part of the shield, to be covered like the shield, but Porter subsequently had two cast iron conical shaped pilot houses made and placed at each end. These were cast hollow in the middle and about twelve inches thick, with four loop holes for observations. They were not used by Commodore Franklin Buchanan during the engagement in Hampton Roads, as he preferred to stand partially exposed in one of the hatchways and communicated his orders to the helmsman.

As the work progressed, Secretary Mallory became very anxious for its speedy conclusion, and on 19 August, a little more than a month after it was begun, he wrote the following order, found in the *Official Records,* which would be followed by a series of others, all bearing increasing anxiety:

Confederate States Navy Department
Richmond, August 19th, 1861

Flag Officer F. Forrest,
Commanding Navy Yard, Gosport

Sir.—The great importance of these services expected of the *Merrimac,* and the urgent necessity of her speedy completion, induces me to call upon you to push forward the work with the utmost dispatch. Chief Engineer Williamson and Constructor Porter, severally in charge of the two branches of this great work, and for which they will be held personally responsible, will receive therefore every possible facility at the expense and delay of every other work on hand if necessary.

S.R. Mallory,
Secretary Confederate States Navy

Mallory's words, ". . . and for which they will be held personally responsible," must have both dismayed Porter as well as delighted him. Now whether the project was a success or failure was completely on the shoulders of Porter and Williamson. As chief naval constructor in supervision over the project, Porter's legacy would rest on a badly burned and previously sunk vessel, the USS *Merrimac(k)* that many declared was already obsolete from stem to stern.

But Porter would not hurry the conversion along any faster than the full capacity of Gosport, which he knew far better than the Confederate Secretary of Navy and the bureaucracy in Richmond. He was clever at keeping the yard commandant informed as he stretched his men and materials, but he was also totally honest at all times about the work that needed to be done to give the men who would become her crew a fighting chance for survival in battle. Familiar with the variety of tactics federal ships would utilize to immobilize and sink his ironclad, Porter conceived a method to protect her rudder and propeller from being rammed. He built a heavy, solid deck, or fantail, extending over them. The fantail was designed to force the enemy to break through it before reaching either the rudder or the propeller. He also added a cast iron ram, or "beak" that weighed about 1,500 pounds. He argued later that he would have preferred that the ram be built as an integral part of the bow rather than a mere attachment. However, pressed for time, he bolted it on the outside of her stem. When the ram was in place, Porter met with Meads and Farmer who agreed with Porter's assessment that the ship was "not built originally with a view to making a ram of her as, they agreed, it would not be safe to do so." Before he was finished, he made sure shipyard commander French Forrest knew about his reservations concerning the ram.

As a safeguard to protect the hull as coal and ammunition were spent in battle, Porter calculated that the *Virginia* would need a course of iron one inch thick fastened all around her exactly three feet down from the knuckle or below the waterline. Many of those around Porter questioned his figures and how he arrived at such a "peculiar arrangement," but as it turned out, he would be proven correct in battle.

Her armament consisted of two 7-inch rifle guns, on pivot, one at each end, utilizing the angle of fire provided by three ports at either end. Her broadsides consisted of eight smooth bore 9-inch Dahlgren guns of her original battery. The 7-inch rifle guns were made at the Tredegar Iron Works in Richmond under the supervision of Brooke who had conducted preliminary tests at Jamestown and Craney Islands. The armor plate was rolled in Richmond at Tredegar Iron Works almost continuously in competition with the infantry's needs. The gun carriages and their block and tackle were made in the shipyard's carpenter shop under the supervision of Porter's brother, Joseph.

Porter always regretted asking more from his workers, although he was working night and day and sleeping over in the yard during the last months of the conversion. However, near the end, and after unrelenting pressure from Richmond, he was finally forced to ask his workmen if they could give more hours. The political alliance Porter's brother Joseph H. Porter had made with the shipyard mechanics 20 years earlier during a labor dispute now proved beneficial. J.W.H. Porter wrote, "The work on the *Merrimac* was hastened with all possible dispatch, and the workmen employed on her evinced a very patriotic spirit. She was a novel kind of a vessel, and they felt a pride in her as the invention of a fellow Portsmouth man. They also maintained a desire to see how she would perform the duty expected of her. In order to expedite the work, the blacksmiths, machinists and bolt drivers signed a voluntary proposition to work until 8 o'clock every night without extra pay.

Not everyone in Gosport offered positive comments to Porter and the workmen as they carried on the conversion. The prevailing opinion among many onlookers was that the ship was top heavy. Critics predicted that once she reached the Elizabeth, she would immediately capsize, turning bottom up. Some referred to Porter behind his back as just a "visionary," while others sneered that he was merely building "an iron coffin" that would certainly drown any crew that dared go aboard. Porter remembered that among the officers stationed at the yard or ordered to the ship, only one, Captain A. B. Fairfax, gave him any encouragement. Even after he reported to Captain S. S. Lee, executive officer of the yard, that the *Virginia* was ready to be floated in drydock on 17 February 1862, Captain Lee was not convinced It was obvious to Porter that on the morning of the 17th, the majority of officers who came to witness the flooding of the dry dock were really there to place wagers that the *Virginia* would fail, thus guaranteeing the survival of wooden hulls and canvass sails. Porter said, "Lieutenant Catesby ap Jones, who was ordered to her as executive officer a short time before she was completed, was among those who expressed a want of faith in her ability to float."

According to Porter's granddaughter, Mrs. A. P. Bailey, (From a September, 1977 interview with the author at the Governor Dinwiddie Hotel, Portsmouth, Virginia) instead of remaining at the drydock on that eventful day to receive the congratulations of those who had doubted him, Porter walked home alone to have his lunch. Earlier, he had politely turned down an opportunity to dine with the shipyard commander at his home in Quarters "A". Those who knew him and passed him that day on the street remembered that he showed no expression of failure or success, but simply nodded in reply to their salutations and sauntered silently onward in that slow, predictable stride of his.

Meanwhile, without fanfare since her constructor was no where to be found, the *Virginia* was moved around to the shipyard's loading wharf to receive some of her ammunition, coal, and supplies. No one on that day realized she would be in the midst of battle in a matter of weeks.

CHAPTER ELEVEN

In His Own Words—The CSS *Virginia*

It is only proper that after so much has been written by so many about the ironclad CSS *Virginia*, that the man who designed and supervised her construction should have his say, word-for-word!

Fortunately Porter began a series of writings in April 1862 that detailed the conversion of the USS *Merrimac(k)* into the ironclad CSS *Virginia*, and her subsequent battles in Hampton Roads. The following Porter memoir is included in its entirety for the first time. Since he was on site during the entire conversion project, his narrative offers the most complete story of the building of the CSS *Virginia* at Gosport shipyard ever written.

Unfortunately a public debate occurred immediately after the CSS *Virginia* was floated in drydock on 17 February, 1862, over the right to claim credit for the invention of the ironclad. The two antagonists were Confederate naval constructor John L. Porter and Confederate naval ordnance officer Lt. John M. Brooke. Porter's argument as the rightful inventor, designer and builder is also included because it offers new information about the CSS *Virginia* that might not have ever been published, and it offers new insight into the personality of Porter, who, by his own admission was surprised by Brooke's public claim. Known to be an unusually quiet man in regard to his professional work, the Brooke claim forced Porter into a series of rare public statements. Even though they offer some repetitive details about the conversion and ensuing battle with the federal fleet and the USS

Monitor, they also illuminate Porter's pride in his achievement. Thus begins his story of the event. Unfortunately the question over who deserves the credit continues to be debated. Porter's first person narrative describing how he conducted the conversion of the USS *Merrimac(k)* into the CSS *Virginia* is, however, a very convincing argument for his claim.

C.S.S. VIRGINIA (MERRIMACK)
Story of Her Construction, Battles, Etc.
By John L. Porter
Naval Constructor
April, 1862

"Shortly after the beginning of the war between the north and south in 1861, I resigned my position as naval constructor in the U.S. service and accepted a similar appointment in the Confederate States service. Seeing the great advantage which the U.S. would have over the Confederate States in the point of a large navy, I concluded I would get up an ironclad vessel for harbor defense, and as I had originated and made a model for that purpose in 1846 in the city of Pittsburgh, Pa., where I was superintending an iron steamer for the U.S. government, I made a facsimile of that model and presented it to Secretary S.R. Mallory of the C.S. Navy at Richmond in May 1861.

"A commission was immediately ordered to take the matter into consideration consisting of Chief Engineer Wm. P. Williamson, Lieutenant J.M. Brooke and Constructor John L. Porter, C.S.N. and after due consideration and from the further fact that we had not the facilities for building steam engines the board unanimously decided that I should cut down the hull of the burnt steamer *Merrimac*, and fit her as an ironclad, putting the shield of my model on her, and submerging her ends and eaves two feet below the water line with inclined sides, as the plan required. This report we submitted to the Navy Department as follows:

Navy Department, Richmond, Va., June 25th, 1861.

Sir—in obedience to your order we have carefully examined and considered the various plans and propositions for constructing a shot proof steam battery, and respectfully report that, in our opinion, the steam frigate *Merrimac,* which is in such condition from the effects of fire as to be useless for any other purpose without incurring a heavy expense in her rebuilding, can be made an efficient vessel of that character, mounting ten heavy guns; two pivot guns, and eight broadside guns of her original battery, and for further consideration, that we cannot procure a suitable engine and boilers for any other vessel without building them, which would occupy too much time, it would appear that this is our only chance to get a suitable vessel in a short time. The bottom of the hull, boilers and heavy and costly parts of the engine, being but little injured, reduce the cost of construction to about one-third the amount which would be required to construct such a vessel anew. We cannot, without further examination, make an accurate estimate of the cost of the projected work, but think it will be about one hundred and ten thousand dollars, the most of which will be for labor, the materials being nearly all on hand in the yard, except the iron plating to cover the shield. The plan to be adopted in the arrangement of her shield for glancing shots, mounting guns, arranging the hull and plating, to be in accordance with the plans submitted for the approval of the department.

                [Signed]   Wm. P. Williamson
                                  Chief Engineer
                          John M. Brooke
                                  Lieutenant
                          John L. Porter
                                  Naval Constructor

"Our report contemplates a plan as being submitted with this report, but as I had no facilities for working drawings in Richmond, there was no plan drawn or submitted at that time, but I returned immediately to the Norfolk Navy Yard and made the first and only plan (the plan or constructor's scroll which measures some 17 feet long and one and 1/2 feet wide is divided into four sections) that ever was made, and forwarded it to the Navy Department, and on the 11th of July it was approved and the following order made out and placed in my hands by the Secretary himself in the Navy Department:

Navy Department
Richmond, Va., July 11th, 1861

Flag Officer F. Forrest:

Sir—You will proceed with all practicable dispatch to make the changes in the *Merrimac,* and to build, equip and fit her in all respects, according to the designs and plans of the Constructor and Engineer, Messrs. Porter and Williamson. As time is of the utmost importance in this matter, you will see that the work progresses without delay to completion.

S.R. Mallory
Secretary Confederate States Navy

"I came immediately back to the navy yard and commenced this great work. Having calculated the weight of the hull as I intended to fit her, with much care, and everything that was to go on her, as armor, guns, machinery, ammunition, stores, coal, shot, and shells, etc., I found that I could cut her hull down to nineteen feet fore and aft, and then have a surplus of fifty tons displacement, but when I drew I found I would cut one foot into her propeller. This I did not wish to do for several reasons, 1st, it would make more (illegible) and consume time, and 2d, it would reduce her speed which I did not wish to do, consequently I raised the line to twenty feet aft, which gave me two hundred tons more than I required for the displacement, which I had to overcome by putting that amount of kentledge (ballast) on her ends and in her spirit room in order to bring her eaves down two feet. Had we had the iron and the time, this amount of weight (illegible) would have been put in the armor, which would have made her more secure.

"Mr. James Meads, who had resigned his appointment as carpenter in the yard, commenced to cut her down in accordance with my directions, and was active in carrying on the work and assisting me until her completion.

"So soon as she was cut down fore and aft, oak knees worked to an angle of thirty-five degrees were fitted between the original frames and bolted into them; to these knees were bolted yellow pine rafters made solid fore and aft the whole length of the shield, and moulded sixteen inches thick. Across these solid rafters a course of yellow pine plank four inches thick was put, fastened and caulked, and across this another course of four inch oak plank was placed up and down on which the armor was placed, making in all a thickness of twenty four inches of solid timber, all caulked.

"The shield was one hundred and fifty feet in length and had four side guns on each side, and one pivot gun in each end, making in all ten guns; eight of these were of her original battery of 9-inch shell guns, Dahlgren patent, and her two pivot guns were of the same plan and size, only they were bored out to seven inches, banded and rifled at the Tredegar works at Richmond, being superintended by Lieutenant John M. Brooke, C.S.N., and were sent to the ship.

"The shield deck was supported by pine beams 10 X 12, and let into the rafters, with oak plank sheer, and an iron gratings covering the entire length made of bars two inches square and meshes 2 X 2.

"The gun deck beams bolted to the shield with large iron knees under them, which knees were taken from the old ship house which the Federals burned. The shield was twenty-four feet long on the inclination and seven feet in height inside.

"When the commission met, we had only intended to put the armor on three inches thick, but Lieutenant Brooke having tried some experiments in Richmond with three thicknesses of one-inch iron, it was found that it would not stand fire at short range, and we concluded to put on four inches, the outside being not less than two inches, upon my assertion that she had displacement enough to bear another inch, which nobody knew but myself. The ram was put on at my own suggestion. Very little was known about them at this time, and for the want of something better to make one out of, we used cast iron; it was fitted to the bow and stern head and bolted strongly to both.

"A great many of the inboard arrangements for capstans,

hauser pipes, steering gear, wheel, etc., had to be of peculiar construction to suit the other arrangements; there were two break waters put on the forward deck to throw off the water, the beams outside of the shield forward and aft were solid and bolted together before the deck was laid; armor one inch thick was placed on these decks, and down the sides below the water line.

"I received but poor encouragement from any of the officers of the navy but one gave me the least, which was Commander (A.B.) Fairfax of the ordnance department; scarcely any of them believed she ever would float which worried me very much at times. Some said if she floated she would turn turtle and would have no stability. I reported to Captain S.S. Lee, the executive officer of the yard, the evening before that I would take her out of the dock the next day. His reply was, 'Mr. Porter do you really think she will float?' But after she had floated successfully they were all satisfied that I knew what I was about, and wrote letters in all directions that she was a success and would do great things.

"Everything being in readiness on Saturday the 8th of March 1862, Captain Franklin Buchanan being in command, Lieutenant Ap Catesby ap Jones, executive officer, she left the navy yard under steam and moved off quite lively towards Newport News, where the U.S. ships *Congress* and *Cumberland* were anchored; she passed up between them delivering her broadsides with terrible effect, and receiving theirs in return, but which had no effect on her whatever, but only glanced off as fast as they struck. She passed up above the ships and attacked the land battery completely silencing it, and then turned and came down on the *Cumberland* and struck her a blow with her ram knocking her bow completely in, which caused her to sink in a short time carrying down most her crew.

"She next made for the *Congress,* which had already struck her colors, and was drifting near the shore where she grounded; she was already on fire and that night blew up with a loud report. Two of the sailing ships attempted to come up from Old Point to the battle ground, but when they saw the fate of the other two ships, they turned and went back again. As the *Merrimack* was nearing the shore on her return at Newport News, Captain Buchanan was wounded by a sharp shooter which was stowed away in the sand on the beach. The *Minnesota* had attempted to

In His Own Words—The CSS Virginia

come up inside the channel from Old Point but grounded and afterwards attacked by the *Merrimack* and the James River flotilla until night brought an end to the fight."

Justifiably proud of his invention, Porter had fully accepted the Confederate Navy's rendition of the battle. However, hearing that the Northern press had pronounced the USS *Monitor* as the victor, he now felt compelled to tell his side of the world's first engagement between ironclads.

"That very evening the *Monitor* was towed into Hampton Roads, and on Sunday the 9th of March she came out to engage the *Merrimack* and after an action of four hours at close range, the *Monitor* retreated to Old Point and never afterwards did she allow the *Merrimack* to get within two miles of her. Lieutenant Jones was then in command and brought the whole flotilla up to the navy yard.

"I then put the *Merrimack* in the dry dock, replaced the broken plates and put more armor on her, refitted her, much improved, armed her with wrought iron slugs, steel pointed instead of cast shells as at first, improved her steering gear, ram, port bucklers, and sent her down the second time under Captain Tattnall much improved.

"Captain Tattnall who succeeded Captain Buchanan (and Catesby ap Jones) in the command took her to Hampton Roads for the express purpose of engaging the *Monitor.* He had made further arrangements with two tugs to board her, jam her turret with iron wedges, stop her ventilation by covering the openings, and forcing a surrender. He also provided extra anchors and cables for the tugs in case the *Monitor* should pull too strong for them so that they could anchor her and prevent her running to Old Point again. But he could not induce her commander to come out from under the guns of Fortress Monroe. He paraded the *Merrimack* up and down but it was no use. There were several merchant vessels lying out there with stores for the U.S. Government, and he sent one of the small gunboats and captured them right in sight but she (*Monitor*) did not come to their relief; the captain of one of the schooners said they were cowards.

"The *Monitor* was never known after the first day's fight to come within range of the *Merrimack's* guns. After we had concluded to evacuate this place to get the troops for the defense of Richmond, and while we were removing our stores, guns, etc. from Sewell's Point, and after all the troops had left, the whole Federal fleet including the *Monitor* came up from Old Point and commenced a heavy cannonade on it.

"The *Merrimack* was sent down to meet them, but just as soon as she hove in sight. The whole of them cut out in double quick, nor did they anchor until they got out side of Fortress Monroe. This does not look much like the *Merrimack* being destroyed by the *Monitor*, yet Lieutenant Worden (commanding officer of USS *Monitor*) and his crew actually made a claim on the U.S. Government for prize money, for having performed that important duty."

At this stage during the brief life of the CSS *Virginia*, Confederate officials argued over what her future should be. It is obvious from Porter's comments that he thought the *Virginia* had a chance to get above the shallows of the James River and contribute to the defense of Richmond along with the other vessels of the James River Fleet. However, his practical mind forced him to advise her commanding officer to take the opposite course.

"It became very evident from events daily happening that we could not hold this station much longer. Captain Tattnall was considering what he should do with the *Merrimack*. She was drawing too much water to go in the James, but thought he would take her to Port Royal where he said he knew of a good harbor, and directed me to have a strong set of port bucklers made and fitted with bars and lanyards to be used in case he took her outside for that purpose, but he never took them out of the carpenter's shop, having as I supposed changed his mind from various reasons. Captain Parrish, the principal pilot on board, related to me the following conversation which he heard while on board, and before her destruction.

"The younger officers advised Captain Tattnall to destroy her, he replied by saying what will become of my reputation; they said to him, 'Commodore your reputation is already established and cannot be hurt.' They stated that there were torpedoes placed between Old Point and the Rip Raps for him, and if he attempted to run by he would be blown up. The pilots had informed him that seventeen feet of water could be carried up the James, and he sent Purser Semple to me to know if she would have stability at that draft. I informed him she would, but it was impossible to get her up to that draft without taking every thing out of her except her machinery, as she was drawing at that time twenty-one feet. This could not be done in sight of the enemy, but they did throw over board about two hundred tons of kentledge to lighten her, then ran her into the bite of Craney Island and on the night of the 10th of May 1862 set her on fire and destroyed her.

"Thus passed away the great ironclad *Merrimack* which had cost so much thought and expense and which had performed such wonderful feats under her gallant commander Buchanan, C.S.N."

CHAPTER TWELVE

The Controversy
A Public Debate Between Brooke and Porter

At this point the Porter memoirs shift to an entirely different focus. Once Confederate ordnance officer Lieutenant John M. Brooke made his public claim as the inventor of the CSS *Virginia*, Porter was forced, against his nature, to reply and present his case to the public with the most detailed answer he could muster. He made this later addition to his original writing on the CSS *Virginia* as part of that defense.

"During the time she was being constructed as an ironclad, I did not know that any other person than myself had responsibility whatever in her plans or success, but to my surprise so soon as she had made such wonderful achievements in Hampton Roads an article appeared in the *Richmond Enquirer* and *Whig* over the signature of Justice written by a Dutchman in Lieutenant Brooke's office claiming for him the planning of the *Merrimack,* which no doubt was done under the cognizance of Lieutenant Brooke.

"When I first carried the model of the shield which was put on the *Merrimack* to Richmond, and before I had ever seen Lieutenant Brooke, Engineer Williamson told me of his aptness to appropriate other people's plans for his own, and warned me against letting him see my plan before I had shown it to Secretary of Navy. I then replied to Justice in the following communication:

John L. Porter

Merrimack or *Virginia*
To the editors of the *Richmond Examiner*

Gosport Navy Yard, March 29, 1862

'Having seen an article in the *Richmond Enquirer* and also one in the *Whig* claiming the plan of the ironclad ship *Virginia* for Lieutenant John M. Brooke of the Navy, thereby doing myself and Engineer Williamson the greatest injustice, I feel called upon to make a statement of facts in the case for the further information of the reading public in the history of this ship.

'In June last Lieutenant Brooke made an attempt to get up a floating battery at the Navy Department. The Secretary sent to this yard for the master ship carpenter to come up and assist him; after trying for a week he failed to produce any thing, and the master carpenter returned to his duties at the yard. Secretary Mallory then sent for me to come to Richmond at which time I carried up the model of an ironclad floating battery with the shield of the present *Virginia* on it, and before I ever saw Lieutenant Brooke; this model may now be seen at the Navy Department.

'The Secretary then ordered a board composed of Engineer Williamson, Lieutenant Brooke and myself to examine, and report upon some plan for a floating ironclad battery. Justice in his communication to the *Whig* says, "After full consultation a plan proposed by Lieutenant John M. Brooke was adopted and received the approval of the Secretary of the Navy, that it was found that the plan of Lieutenant Brooke could easily be applied to the *Merrimack* and in fact no other plan could have made the *Merrimack* an effective ship, and that a report was made to the Secretary of the Navy in accordance with these facts." Now I would only ask a careful reading of this report (June 25, 1861, previously given) and see how far it agrees with the statements of Justice.

'Now I would ask what becomes of the statement of Justice, and I would also ask any one at all acquainted with the circumstances, how Lieutenant Brooke could have had anything to do with this report further than signing his name to it; what did he know about the condition of the *Merrimack* or her engines, or whether there was enough of her left to make a floating battery or not, or anything about her, what it would cost, or anything else about her, for he had not even seen her, and knew nothing of her condition really.

'The concluding part of the report states that the whole arrangements were to be made in accordance with the plan submitted. The facts are that no plan was submitted with the report, after the report was made. I immediately returned to the Norfolk Navy Yard, and made the plans of the Virginia myself, and unaided by any one placed the very same shield on her that was on the model I carried up with me before this board met. On the 11th of July I returned to Richmond with this drawing, and presented it to Secretary Mallory.

'Lieutenant Brooke is not even hinted at in this letter. After the ship had been in progress for six weeks, the Secretary wrote the following letter to Flag-Officer Forrest on the subject.

> Confederate States Navy Department
> Richmond, August 19, 1861
>
> Flag-Officer F. Forrest, commanding Navy Yard,
> Gosport, Va.
>
> Sir: The great importance of the service expected from the *Merrimack*, and the urgent necessity of her speedy completion, induce me to call upon you to push forward the work with the utmost dispatch.
>
> Chief Engineer Williamson, and Constructor Porter severally in charge of two branches of this great work and for which they will be held personally responsible will receive therefore every possible facility at the expense and delay of every other work on hand if necessary.
>
> S. R. Mallory,
> Secretary Confederate States Navy

'Of the great and skillful calculations of the displacements and weights of timber and iron involved in the planning and construction of this great piece of naval architecture, and of her present weight with everything on board, no other man than myself has, or ever had any knowledge; if he has let him show it, for while public opinion said she never would float, no one save myself knew to the contrary, or what she was capable of bearing. After the *Merrimack* was in progress sometime, Lieutenant Brooke was constantly proposing alterations in her to the Secretary of the Navy, and as constantly and firmly opposed by myself, which the Secretary knows.

'To Engineer Williamson who had the exclusive control of the machinery, great credit is due for having improved the propeller and engines as to improve the speed of the ship three knots per hour. I never thought for a moment that after the many difficulties I had to encounter in making these new and intricate arrangements for the working of this novel kind of ship, that any one would attempt to rob me of my just merits, for if there was any other man than myself who had the responsibility about her success or failure I never knew it, only so far as the working of the machinery was concerned, for which Engineer Williamson was alone responsible. I hope these plain statements of facts will satisfy the people of this government as to who is entitled to the plan of the *Virginia*.

John L. Porter
C.S.N. Constructor

"The above communication was published right under Lieutenant Brooke's eye, but he did not dare to contradict one word of it, or make any reply to it whatever, and when every thing connected with her was fresh on the minds of all."

Porter then felt compelled to reply to an article published in the April 4, 1862, edition of the (Richmond) *Examiner.* Once again the Porter article, like those earlier, revealed more details about the construction of the CSS *Virginia* which might not have come to light had there not been such a controversy. Entitled, "Who Planned the *Virginia,*" Porter sent his article in the form of a letter to the editor of the *Examiner.*

"Under this caption in the *Examiner* of the 4th instant I find a report of the Secretary of the Navy to Congress giving a detailed statement of the origin of the ironclad *Virginia.* I feel sorry to have to reply to this report in as much as it is published over the signature of the Secretary, and my friends will not fail to see the embarrassing position it places me in, in consequence of my relations with the Navy Department; and furthermore, my intercourse with the Secretary since I held my present position in the Southern Confederacy, has been of the most friendly kind, but justice to myself requires that I should reply to it.

"The report commences by stating 'that on the 10th of June Lieutenant Brooke was directed to aid the department in designing an ironclad war vessel, and framing the necessary specifications, and in a few days submitted to the Department a rough drawing of a casemated vessel, with submerged ends and inclined plated sides, the ends of the vessel and the eaves to be submerged two feet. I do not doubt the statements of the Secretary, but no such plans were submitted to the board, and from the fact that the master carpenter had returned to this yard without completing any plan as the vessel shows, and myself being sent for immediately, and from the further fact that the Secretary presented us no plans from this source, I stated in my last communication that Lieutenant Brooke failed to produce any thing, after a week's trial, and I am still of that opinion so far as any thing tangible is concerned.'

"The report states that the practical mechanic who was brought up from Norfolk was unable to make the drawings for Lieutenant Brooke, and the Department then ordered Chief Engineer Williamson and Constructor Porter from the Navy Yard at Norfolk to Richmond about the 23rd of June for consultation on the same subject generally, and to aid in the work.

"I do not understand this part of the report exactly, but if it is intended to convey the idea that we were to examine any plan of Lieutenant Brooke's I never so understood it, neither did we act in accordance with any such idea as our report will show. The report next refers to my model which I carried up with me, the shield and plan of which is carried out on the *Virginia,* but the report seems to have lost sight of the fact that the eaves and ends of my model were submerged two feet precisely like the *Virginia,* the ship was cut down on a straight line fore and aft, to suit this arrangement, and the shield extended over her just as far as the space inside would admit to work the guns. Where the shield stopped a strong deck was put in to finish out the ends and plated over with iron, and a rough breakwater built on it to throw the water forward.

"The report states that Mr. Porter approved the plan of submerged ends, and made a clear drawing of Lieutenant Brooke's plan which that officer then filed with the Department. How could I disapprove of my own model which had submerged ends and eaves two feet, and the only drawing I ever made of the *Virginia* was made at my office in this navy yard and which I presented to the Department on the 11th of July, just sixteen days after this board adjourned, having been ordered to Richmond on other business. This drawing and plan I considered my own, and not Lieutenant Brooke's. So soon as I presented this plan the Secretary wrote the following order while everything was fresh in his mind concerning the whole matter.

> Navy Department
> Richmond, July 11, 1861
>
> Flag-Officer French Forrest,
>
> Sir: you will proceed with all practicable dispatch to make the changes in the form of the *Merrimack* and to build, equip and fit her in all respects according to the design and plans of the constructor and engineer Messrs. Porter and Williamson.
>
> S.R. Mallory
> Secretary, C.S. Navy

"What, I would ask, could be more explicit than this letter, or what words could have established my claim stronger if I had dictated them. The concluding part of this report says, 'The novel plan of submerging the ends of the ship and the eaves of the casemate however is the peculiar and distinctive feature of the *Virginia.*' This may all be true, but it is just what my model calls for, and if Lieutenant Brooke presented rough drawings to the Department carrying out the same views it may be called a singular coincidence, and here I would remark that my model was not calculated to have much speed, but was intended for harbor defense only, and was of light draft, the eaves extending over the entire length of the model, and submerged all around two feet, ends and sides and the line on which I cut the ship down was just in accordance with this, but if Lieutenant Brooke's ideas which were submitted to the Secretary in his rough drawings had been carried out to cut her ends down low enough to build tanks to regulate the draft of the vessel, she would have been cut much lower than my plan required, for all the water which now covers her ends would not alter her draft three inches if confined in tanks. All the calculations of the weights and displacements, and the line to cut the ship down were determined by myself, as well as her whole arrangements.

"That Lieutenant Brooke may have been of great assistance to the Department in trying the necessary experiments in determining the thickness of the armor, getting up her battery, and attending to the shipping of the iron, etc., I do not doubt; but to claim for him the credit of designing the ship, is a matter of too much interest to me to give up.

"Engineer Williamson discharged his duties with great success, the engines performed beyond his most sanguine expectations and these with the improvements in her propeller have increased her speed three miles per hour. The Confederacy is under many obligations to Secretary Mallory for having approved the report of this board in making (illegible) a bomb proof ship; her performance has changed the whole system of naval defenses so far as wooden ships are concerned. Europe as well as America will have to begin anew, and that nation which can produce ironclad ships with the greatest rapidity will be the mistress of the seas.

"In this communication I disclaim any disrespect to the Secretary of the Navy whatever; he has not only been my friend in this government, but was a true and serviceable one under the U.S. Government, and has rendered me many acts of kindness for which I have always esteemed him, but the present unpleasant controversy involves a matter of so much importance to me, that I shall be excused for defending my claim not only as the constructor but the originator of the plan of the *Virginia*."

John L. Porter
Confederate States Navy Constructor

After these kind statements about Secretary of Navy Mallory, Porter sharply criticized Mallory for accepting Brooke's argument about the design. In this notation, Porter began to use his plans and model as his best defense, which should have been sufficient evidence to win his side of the argument. One has to wonder why Porter did not more often use his constructor's scroll of conversion drawings as conclusive evidence for his side of the argument during the debate.

It is evident that Secretary Mallory made a most unfair report to Congress. He says the distinctive features of the *Merrimack* were her submerged ends and eaves, and yet in speaking of my model he studiously avoids to mention that fact, and says not a word about it although the model was in his office, and right before his eyes; furthermore why was it that the rough drawings of Lieutenant Brooke were so soon lost, or were not produced if he had any which would have proved the correctness of his statement if he had any, they were not like the *Merrimack*.

J.L.P
N.C.

Thus ends one of the more depressing moments of Porter's life as Chief Confederate Naval Constructor. The so-called Brooke-Porter controversy, that became so public during the war, left permanent scars on both sides of the Brooke and Porter families for generations to come and has divided historians ever since.

High Street, 1872. Looking west from a point near Crawford

Monumental Methodist Church

John L. Porter

The Navy Yard at Portsmouth, Virginia

The Norfolk Navy Yard is one of the best in the United States. It is provided with all the usual furniture of a navy-yard-ship houses, storehouses, foundries, etc., and has besides, a granite dock which costs millions of dollars. At this navy-yard is anchored, as receiving ship, the old *Pennsylvania,* the largest line-of-battleship in the world. She is shown in the foreground of the picture.

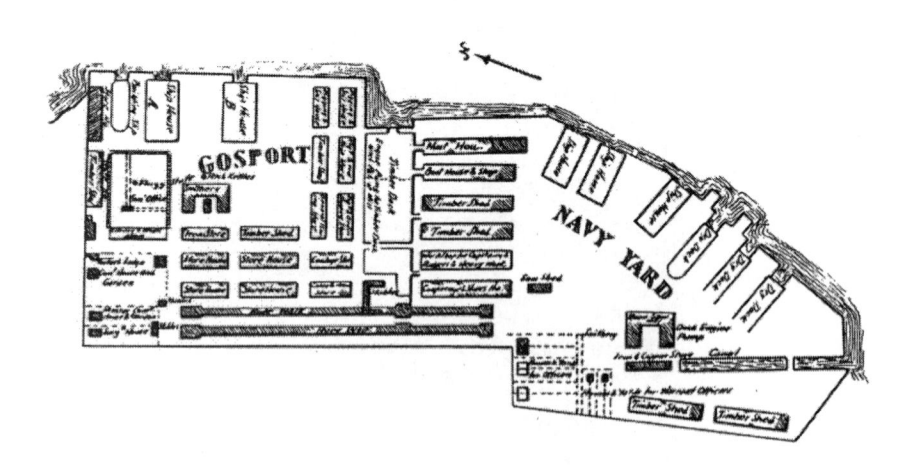

Plan of Gosport Navy Yard 1851

USS *Merrimac(k)*

CSS *Merrimac(k)* at the burning of Gosport, April 19, 1861

John L. Porter

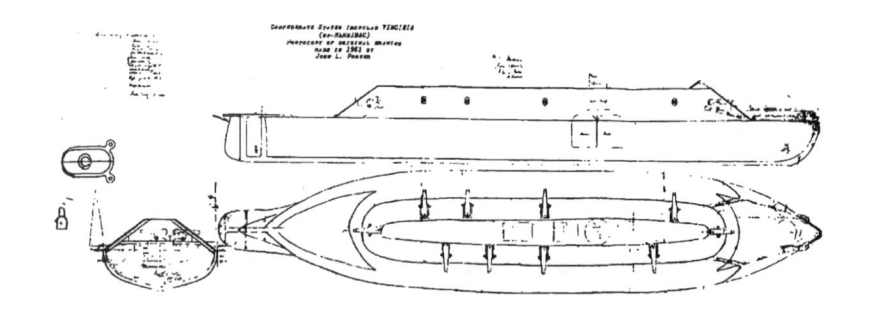

1861 drawing of C.S. Ironclad *Virginia* by John L. Porter

USS *Merrimac(k)* in dry dock, being converted into CSS *Virginia*

John L. Porter

Blackford's sketch of the CSS *Virginia*, 1862

CSS *Virginia* sinking USS *Cumberland*, March 8, 1862

John L. Porter

Porter letter to Reverend Moore
with rough sketch of the CSS *Virginia*

CSS *Virginia* battling USS *Monitor,* March 9, 1862

John L. Porter

Portsmouth raising the Stars and Stripes, June 1862

James Gardner photograph of the ruins of Gosport, Portsmouth, Virginia, 1864

CHAPTER THIRTEEN

Battle of Hampton Roads

The next portion of the Porter memoir contains his summary of how the CSS *Virginia* fought in the Battle of Hampton Roads and the subsequent loss of Gosport, which led to the ironclad's destruction. Once again Porter was determined to get the entire story out including some criticisms about *Virginia*'s officers that have never been published before.

"After the actions of the *Merrimack* on the 8th and 9th of March 1862, she was put in the dry dock, and refitted and improved in her armor, etc., and Captain Josiah Tattnall, C.S. Navy, took her to Hampton Roads for the express purpose of engaging the *Monitor*, but that vessel could not be induced to come from under the guns of Fortress Monroe. Captain Tattnall sent a small gunboat and captured a merchantman with stores for the Fortress, right under her guns, but it was no go, nor ever afterwards did she come within range of *Merrimack's* guns.

"On the 9th of May 1862, a man (Yankee) in the employ of the Confederacy, and commanding a tug which was engaged in bringing up stores from Sewells Point battery, deserted and informed General Wool, U.S.A. at Fortress Monroe, that the Confederates were evacuating this station, when the Federal fleet came up and commenced to bombard it, the gunners had all left. The *Merrimack* went down to meet them, but just as soon as she rounded Pinners Point they all cut out, *Monitor* and all, nor did

89

they stop until they got outside of Old Point, and didn't let her get within two miles of them.

"On the 10th day of May 1862 everything being in readiness, the navy yard was fired and evacuated by the Confederate troops. On that night Captain Tattnall having had all the kentledge ballast thrown overboard from the *Merrimack,* ran her into the bite of Craney Island, and destroyed her by fire, she drawing too much water to take her up the James River, but she was not destroyed by the *Monitor,* as was claimed by some, but was in complete fighting trim when she was destroyed, and vastly superior to that of her two days' fights in Hampton Roads.

"There is no doubt but that the Federals stood in perfect dread of the *Merrimack.* It is a well known fact that they never came within reach of her guns after the fight on the 9th of March 1862. After she was refitted and taken to Hampton Roads by Captain Josiah Tattnall C.S.N., she steamed up and down and challenged the *Monitor* to come out but she would not move from under the guns of Fortress Monroe, and on the 9th day of May when the Confederates were preparing to evacuate this station (which they did the next day) she ran the whole Federal fleet from Sewells Point battery, whither they had come to bombard it, after the troops had been withdrawn, nor did they anchor until they had passed outside of Fortress Monroe, the *Monitor* included. I heard that the U.S. Navy Department shared in the same dread, and had issued orders to her commander not to engage the *Merrimack* again if he could prevent it, for he said if she was captured they would have no showing in these waters."

The final portion of the Porter memoir is in the form of a letter he wrote on December 21, 1874, to Commander Thomas O. Selfridge, U.S.N., who was then stationed at the Boston Navy Yard and working on his own memoir about his time onboard the USS *Congress* during the battle with the *Virginia.* The seven-page typed transcript is a highly detailed account of Porter's perspective of the Battle of Hampton Roads and his refitting of the *Virginia* afterwards. It also marked the last time Porter would write formally about the ironclad.

"Sir: Mr. George R. Boush, Assistant Naval Constructor at this navy yard, has called on me and presented your letter of the

14th instant, asking for certain information in regard to the *Merrimack, Monitor,* etc., which I cheerfully give from the fact 'that you state as a matter of history you want the facts to set the history straight.'

"There is no matter that I know of in which so may erroneous statements have been made from time to time, and in fact I must say that I have yet to see the first correct one published.

"Having constructed the *Merrimack* as an ironclad, docked her after the action in Hampton Roads, and refitted her in the dock at the Gosport Navy Yard, noticing every particular of the condition of the ship, and the effects from the shots of the various ships with which she was engaged, and also being fully acquainted with the particular of those engagements, I am fully capable of giving you the desired information, and also other interesting facts in connection with her history, which you do not ask, but which I think will interest you, and which no other person has, all of which are strictly true, to which I would qualify.

"The *Merrimack* was armed with eight 9-inch shell guns in her broadside of her original battery, and one 7-inch rifled gun in each end of the shield mounted on a pivot carriage. As we did not expect to encounter any ironclad, she was only provided with shells for all her guns, rifled and smooth bore.

"She left the navy yard at one o'clock on Saturday the 8th of March, 1862, and steamed for Newport News, where the *Congress* and *Cumberland* were lying at anchor; the *Congress* on the starboard side, and the nearest, received the first fire; a shell from the bow gun entered her stern port on the spar deck and killed Lieutenant Smith, U.S.N. She very soon came abreast of the *Congress* and received her broadside which made no impression whatever, that could be noticed inside the casemate.

"She continued on, and very soon came abreast of a land battery, and opened her fire upon it for some time upsetting every thing in it. She then turned and came down on the *Cumberland* striking her a glancing blow with her ram which carried her bow in, and at the same time broke off the ram which was made of cast iron, and projected the stem two feet. (Here Porter included a rough drawing of the ram and how it was attached to the bow.) It was made thus the weight of which did not exceed one ton. The breaking off caused a small leak at the stem but hardly perceptible, not making a barrel of water in twenty-four hours, and which was the only leak she ever had. The *Cumberland* soon went down bow foremost.

"The *Congress* had already struck her colors and was (by port shot) set on fire. Captain Franklin Buchanan, her commander, was stationed in a small hatch way with the pilot Captain Parrish all the time and did not receive any injury from the fire of shot or shells from the *Congress, Cumberland* or land battery, although his head and shoulders were exposed, but on nearing the shore at Newport News, some of the sharpshooters fired into his ports killing one or two of his men, and from his position he could see them and calling for a musket, he fired on them, but not having room he impudently got out of his position upon the shield and was wounded. No shot or shell penetrated her shield in any of the actions and the only men who were killed were those mentioned above.

"Lieutenant Robert Minor was flag lieutenant, and after the firing from the ships had ceased, made an examination all round and reported to Captain Buchanan that they had not fazed her (to use his own words); this he related to me himself. The ship then passed down towards the *Minnesota,* U.S. steamer. The C.S. gunboats *Jamestown* and *Teaser* which had been fitted out at Richmond came out of the James early in the action and fought throughout on the first day, but not with the *Monitor.* So soon as the firing began by the *Merrimack* the U.S. steamer *Minnesota* which was laying off Fortress Monroe got underway and attempted to go up to Newport News by the inside channel and grounded; she was in this condition when the *Merrimack* came down the outside channel. Hampton bar being between them, the *Merrimack* neared her until she grounded also, both ships firing rapidly as possible at each other, the shot from the *Merrimack* doing great damage, while those from the *Minnesota* did none whatever.

"This continued until night came on and put a stop to the fight for the 1st day, the 8th of March 1862. On that very evening the *Monitor* was towed into Hampton Roads, and that night the magazine of the *Congress* blew up with a tremendous noise which was the last of a noble ship.

"On Sunday morning (9 March 1862) the *Monitor* came out to engage the *Merrimack.* Up to this time the *Merrimack* had sustained no injury except the breaking off the ram in the *Cumberland* and the shooting off of the muzzle of a broadside gun, but which did not prevent its use.

"The action lasted several hours, the vessels at times touching each other, and with no seeming advantage to either, (but in my opinion had the *Merrimack* been provided with solid shot and slugs, steel pointed as she was afterwards, the result would have been different) until a shell struck the lookout on the *Monitor* immediately in front of Lieutenant John L. Worden, U.S.N., commanding her, and who was directing the fight, and knocked him senseless from the concussion. (Worden was partially blinded.)

"So soon as this occurred the *Monitor* cut for Old Point, and Lieutenant Catesby Ap Jones C.S.N., who then commanded the *Merrimack* made signal for all the vessels to go up to the navy yard. This course of Lieutenant Jones was not generally sustained. Captain Buchanan said to me afterwards that Jones had made a great mistake in not going for the *Minnesota*. The only good reason I could see for his coming up was that his vessel had been lightened so much from the burning of her coals, and the discharge of shells and powder as to bring her vulnerable parts near the surface forward, but aft she was more secure, as her propeller and steering gear were submerged deeper, the ship having tipped by the stern.

"I saw the assistant surgeon of the *Minnesota* in Baltimore afterwards who told me that the officers and crew of the ship all left her on Saturday night, the 8th of March, and went to Fortress Monroe and held a consultation and concluded that they would send a few men on board of her on Sunday morning with directions if the *Merrimack* made an attack on her again to set her on fire and retreat; a small party was consequently sent on board for that purpose, but just as soon as the *Merrimack* left the Roads, the crew went on board again, got up steam and got her off. This I witnessed myself. (Porter probably watched from the Confederate batteries at Sewell's Point, or perhaps with the aid of a telescope from Craney Island.)

"The next day, Monday the 10th, I put her in the dry dock, made a thorough examination, and found no serious damage anywhere. I put a piece in the stem and put on a better ram of wrought iron and steel extending back on the bow about fourteen feet. I found eight or ten plates broken in the shield by the shot from the *Monitor*, but none of the plates were knocked off. I could tell these shots very easily from the shots of the other ships because two were fired (close) together, and being at close range they invariably struck the shield close to each other, and low down, both being ten inch solid shot. The effect of the two I considered far more destructive than one would have been. These plates I soon replaced, and without the least difficulty. I examined the whole shield outside and counted ninety indentations made from the shots of the other ships, and twenty made by the shots from the *Monitor* which were the only ones which did any damage or broke a plate. These plates were eight inches wide and two inches thick, put on in two thicknesses; none of the inner courses were removed. "What detained the ship so long in dock was, we were putting on more armor, so as to protect her better near the water's edge. (At this point in the memoir, Porter included a drawing of how the armor was attached to the shield.) We bent more iron two inches thick and bolted it over the ends of the inclined plating for better protection in case she was lightened, we were also making wrought iron slugs with steel points for all her guns which she was fully supplied when she went down to meet the *Monitor* the second time. We also improved her steering gear, and she was a much better ship.

"Captain Tattnall was in command and he took her to Hampton Roads for the express purpose of meeting the *Monitor*, and waited for her to come out but she failed to do so. There were several small vessels with stores for the U.S. Government lying out there. Captain Tattnall sent one or two small gun boats and captured them right under her guns, and brought them to the navy yard, but she still remained under the guns of Old Point, and never afterwards did she come within the range of the *Merrimack*'s guns.

"Furthermore when afterwards we were preparing to evacuate this place, and were removing all the guns from Sewells Point battery, a man in our service in charge of a tug deserted and carried the news to General Wool, U.S. army at Fortress Monroe when the whole Federal fleet got under way and commenced a rapid fire on it, including the *Monitor*, but we had no men there to reply, but the *Merrimack* was sent down from the yard (Gosport) to meet the whole fleet, but just as soon as she rounded Pinners Point, and hove in sight, the whole fleet, *Monitor* and all, cut out for Fortress Monroe and didn't let the *Merrimack* get within two miles of them.

"I heard afterwards that her commander had orders from the Navy Department, to avoid another fight with the *Merrimack* if possible on account of the great stakes at issue, for it was plain if either of them were out of the way, the other would have the control of these waters. I never supposed for a moment that her officers were not brave, but at any rate it does not look much like she was destroyed by the *Monitor*, as I understand Admiral Worden is claiming prize money. The cause of her destruction was the advance of General McClellan on Richmond; this place had to be evacuated to get troops, and as we could not get her in the James, on account of her draft of water, she would have been in the Federal lines and cut off from supplies, and would have been compelled to surrender very soon. Captain Tattnall thought his only chance was to destroy her. At one time he thought of taking her to Port Royal, and I actually had a strong set of port bucklers and bars made for that purpose, but he changed his mind. When destroyed (completed during the early morning hours of May 11), she was in fighting trim, and vastly superior to that in her two days' fight."

Your respectfully,
John L. Porter
Naval Constructor

Almost one month before the Confederate evacuation of Gosport, General John B. Magruder, then in charge of defending the Virginia Peninsula and preventing Federal advancement towards Richmond, sharply criticized the management of Gosport and Porter, in particular, for their slowness in completing the *Virginia*. Captain Sidney S. Lee, Gosport's second Confederate commander after French Forrest and brother of General Robert E. Lee, took strong objection in his April 8, 1862 report to Secretary Mallory. The report is also valuable because it sheds light on how difficult it was to work the *Virginia*'s iron and port shutters. A copy can be found in the *Official Records* as follows:

"Sir: Herewith I enclose a letter from Mr. Porter, in reply to extracts with which he was furnished from General Magruder's letter of the 3d to the Secretary of War, relative to the 'criminal neglect' in fitting the Virginia for service. In justice to all concerned, I beg leave to state that no time was lost in preparing the ship; the work was prosecuted every day in the week, Sundays included, and on occasion all night. The labor of putting on the iron is immense and tedious, as the bars are very heavy and but few men can get at them to work on the stages. In short, the ship has gone down with everything done for her that was required, except putting on her port shutters and the iron below her water line, which was partially finished.

"The broadside ports are now in hand, and were only required on the 3d; at least, I never heard that they were intended to be put on until that date. The commodore (Franklin Buchanan), on the morning of that day, spoke to me of them and expressed a wish to have them fitted. I put them in the smith shop forthwith to be fitted up. Each shutter has to be adjusted to its respective port. We finished those for the head and stern ports and they worked satisfactorily, and were going on with the bow, quarter, and broadside shutters when the ship was undocked. Some additional iron arrived yesterday and will at once be prepared for use. No requisitions tending to promote the public interests or supply the squadron in a proper manner have at any time been neglected. The officers of the *Virginia* were specially consulted as her repairs progressed.

"In view of the facts here stated, and those laid before the Department by Mr. Porter, I feel assured that this yard and its officers will stand acquitted of the hasty impeachments contained in General Magruder's letter, which, as you will observe, were based on erroneous and imperfect information."

Thus ended Porter's CSS *Virginia* and his days at Confederate-held Gosport. He now faced the challenge of coordinating the building of an ironclad navy around the coast and on the riverbanks of the Confederacy whose very days, he knew, were numbered. His fearful prediction that the Confederacy did not have an industrial base large enough to sustain the war was about to be proven true.

The loss of Gosport was a major blow to the morale of the Confederate Navy as well as to Porter personally. He had grown up along the Elizabeth River and earned his apprenticeship at Gosport and at his father's shipyard nearby. He had established his own home and family in the city and county in which the Porters had served for over two centuries. The evacuation of Gosport meant uprooting his family once more, and this time sending them to Richmond, where he knew the Federal campaign on the Virginia Peninsula was headed. But leaving them in Portsmouth while he took offices in the Confederate Navy Department in Richmond was impossible. He was certain there would be repercussions during the Federal reoccupation of Portsmouth. He feared that if his family was found to belong to the man who built the *Virginia*, they would be targeted for harassment if not arrest. In quiet family meetings before their departure to Richmond, he began to prepare them for what he knew all along was inevitable. If he was forced into a life on the run following the Confederacy's defeat, various Porter relations pledged to support his family until he could return. Porter's decision about their removal to Richmond was made at the end of April 1862, following a visit by Secretary Mallory, who informed shipyard commander Captain Sidney Lee that the yard was to be evacuated. But, before all of that, there were ironclads and gunboats to design and build.

CHAPTER FOURTEEN

Building a Confederate Navy

During the Confederate occupation of Gosport, Porter had also designed a series of what became known as "Maury" gunboats that, in addition to a series of "Porter-style" gunboats, could be quickly built in large enough numbers to threaten the blockading fleet around Hampton Roads and points further south. A December 4, 1862 letter, now in the University of North Carolina archives, from steam engineer Williamson to Confederate naval constructor Gilbert Elliott at Elizabeth City, North Carolina, offers some description of the gunboats and interesting insight into the control Porter had over Confederate naval construction in general.

Williamson wrote, "I am sorry to hear that you find the last drafts as objectionable as the first. The beam being 25 ft instead of 30 ft, on the same draft, certainly makes the midshipsection 1/5 less, consequently the resistance is decreased in that ratio. The lines are also finer and as the engines are the same in both, the last model must be the most speedy.

"As I am already in a scrape by objecting to Mr. Porter's plans and have really no right to interfere with them, I cannot do so again. My object before was to reconcile the difficulty you labored under, between Mr. Porter's model and Capt. Lynch's contract. The Secretary gives Mr. Porter whole control in the designs of the hulls and unless you can exhibit to him a better model and gain his approval thereto, the whole control rests with Mr. Porter.

"In regard to the 50 gun boats now wanted, Mr. Porter made the drawings. They are 106 ft long, 21 ft beam and 8 ft deep. These designs have been accepted by the Navy. The engines are all to be alike in size and design and I am now hunting up the various engine builders in the Confederacy to undertake the work.

"Mr. Porter will, I presume, have the same authority with regard to the hulls, so if you desire to build them, you had better communicate with him on the subject."

In a series of communications with Mallory, also in the University of North Carolina archives, Porter described the machinery and armament requirements of his gunboats. He recommended two non-condensing engines with 16-inch diameter cylinders, and 20-inch piston strokes. They were also equipped with two boilers with 800 feet of fire surface each, and two return flues. To produce extra speed, they were propelled by two three-bladed screw propellers of seven feet diameter and twelve feet pitch mounted on wrought iron shafts. Porter further designed the gunboats to carry two broadside carriage-mounted rifled guns of four-inch bore. Writing that a larger six-inch bore be mounted at the bow, Porter proposed that an experienced crew could roll the heavier gun to the stern port to cover the rear as well.

The priority Confederate Navy Secretary Mallory placed on Porter's gunboats is well evidenced by a March 19, 1862 order from him to the Gosport Shipyard commander, Captain French Forrest, that is found in the *Official Records.*

"Sir: The completion of the ironclad gunboat being constructed at the yard is a matter of the first consequence, and a moment must not be lost in accomplishing it. As many men must be kept at work upon her by day, and by night if practicable, as can be usefully employed. You will immediately direct Constructor Porter to employ the private builders at and near Norfolk who are constructing gunboats for us, and aid him in every way to push forward this vessel if you can thereby expedite her completion. You will also direct Major [Engineer] Williamson to have the engines ready for this vessel in time, and make every exertion to complete them. One such vessel would be worth a fleet of wooden vessels to us."

A second order concerning gunboats quickly followed from Mallory to Forrest on 30 March 1862 that is also part of the *Official*

Records. This particular order, besides emphasizing the urgency of completion, serves to underscore the close working relationship Porter had established with Williamson on almost every important project. No doubt some of the commentary that follows must have vexed Porter, particularly the part referring to employing "one hundred or a thousand more," as the yard was as deficient in manpower as it was in critical materials.

"Sir: You are specially requested to urge on the completion of the ironclad gunboat in course of construction. The engines and boilers should be in place, her ordnance stores ready, her crew shipped and exercised, and the vessel prepared for action without the loss of an hour. All the preparations should progress simultaneously.

"Advertise for mechanics in North Carolina, if you need them, and employ one hundred or a thousand or more if necessary, but push on the work.

"You are also specially directed to urge with all possible dispatch the completion of the small ironclad gunboats designed for the North Carolina waters, and to go through the Albemarle Canal. Call upon Constructor Porter, get his plans and specifications, and set him at work, by contract or otherwise, upon them immediately. Say eight such vessels, to carry at least two heavy guns, and not to draw, when ready for service, over 5 1/2 or 6 feet. Proceed to work without the loss of a day. Chief Engineer Williamson will furnish the motive power.

"Stimulate your workers by every means in your power, and if you want more officers, or desire the detachment of any you have, for the good of the service, you are requested to suggest them.

"The Department desires to do all in its power to develop the full powers of the yard."

Even though the time he had at Gosport was short and the additional pressure from Richmond was on the increase, Porter managed to design and supervise the construction of several gunboats in addition to the ironclads CSS *Virginia* and *Richmond*. The 80-ton gunboats CSS *Nansemond* and *Hampton*, each carrying two guns, were launched in time to steam up the James and take part in the defense of Richmond. But five others were not so fortunate. The unfinished Confederate gunboats *Norfolk,*

Portsmouth, Escambia, Elizabeth and *Yadkin* were burned on 10 May 1862 to prevent capture.

By the spring of 1862, Gosport was not secure enough for further construction of smaller ironclads either. Porter watched with grave disappointment as eight small, flat-bottomed ironclads, called the "Dismal Swamp" ironclads for their ability to traverse the Dismal Swamp Canal from Portsmouth to the North Carolina sounds, were scrapped. Each had been designed to carry two guns and was, along with his series of light draft gunboats, his solution to counteract the larger blockading United States Navy. Porter had just finished negotiating a contract on April 16, 1862, with North Carolina ship builder Gilbert Elliott to construct a new ironclad when it too had to be destroyed before completion during that terrible May of 1862. This event further underscored for Porter what he had predicted all along.

Fortunately, for the Confederate Navy, Porter had been busy planning, designing, and negotiating with shipbuilders throughout the Confederacy and in England. This relationship produced a string of highly innovative new ironclads that were much advanced over his prototype CSS *Virginia*.

For its time, Porter's 150-foot, four-gun CSS *Richmond*, built at Gosport, 6 May 1861, was one of the most advanced ironclads of the war. She was so well received that her design spawned a series of *Richmond*-class ironclads including the CSS *Raleigh*, built by J.L. Cassidy, Wilmington, North Carolina, CSS *North Carolina*, built by Berry and Bros., Wilmington, North Carolina, CSS *Chicora*, built by James M. Eason, Charleston, South Carolina, CSS *Palmetto State*, Cameron and Co., Charleston, South Carolina, and CSS *Savannah*, Henry F. Willink, Savannah, Georgia.

Coordination between Porter, who drew the plans at Gosport, and shipbuilder Gilbert Elliot at Edwards Ferry on the Roanoke River, North Carolina, produced the 139-foot, 2 gun, twin-screw, CSS *Albemarle*. She was commissioned on 17 April, 1864, and two days later, with her two 6.4-inch muzzle-loading rifles, lead the attack on Union forces at Plymouth, N.C. While under repair, she was torpedoed and sunk during a daring night time raid led by Lieutenant W. B. Cushing, 27-28 October 1864. *Albemarle* was subsequently raised by Union forces and returned to the

Gosport shipyard (the yard was renamed the Norfolk Navy Yard after the Civil War) on 27 April 1865 and condemned as a prize. Two years later she was sold.

Albemarle's sister, CSS *Neuse*, was also built on Porter's plan that gave her a 152-foot length, a 34-foot beam, and a draft of 9-feet. Launched by Elliot Smith and Company at Kinston, North Carolina, on the Neuse River in November 1863, she also carried two 6.4-inch muzzle-loading rifles. Her career was brief after she grounded off Kinston and remained fast until March 1865 when she was burned by Confederates to prevent capture by Union army Major General William W. T. Sherman.

While at Rockett's shipyard, Richmond, Porter drew the plans for the 170-foot, four-gun, twin screw, CSS *Fredericksburg*. Launched in November 1863, she was an enlarged version of the highly praised *Albemarle*. She took a 40-foot, three-inch beam, and required a draft of nearly 10 feet. Carrying a complement of 150 officers and crew, her armament consisted of an 11-inch smooth bore, one 8-inch muzzle-loading rifle, and one 6.4-inch muzzle-loading rifle.

During the defense of Richmond, Porter was able to hear daily how the *Fredericksburg* performed with CSS *Richmond* and other consorts against the Union fleet as it pushed up the James in coordination with land-based Federal forces. She could have been somewhat of a disappointment to him as her engagements proved inconclusive.

One of the strangest tales concerning any Porter-designed ironclad was that of the CSS *Mississippi*. Carrying a tonnage of 1,400, and a length of 260-feet, she required a draft of only 12 and 1/2 feet. Her armament was to be one of the most formidable of the war with plans for 20 guns including 4.7-inch pivots at bow and stern. To make her an impregnable battery, Porter's plans demanded 1,000 tons of armor plate rolled at Schofield and Markham iron works in Atlanta with the bolts alone weighing another 80 short tons. Her plating ranged from 1 1/4-inch to 3 3/4-inches. When added to the wooden backing, they contributed to a hull thickness of 2-feet at the sides and 3-feet at bow and stern. Despite her dimension, she was built for speed with three trip screw propellers.

Begun on 14 October 1861, by N. and A.F. Tift in a shipyard

created for her construction at Jefferson City, Louisiana, *Mississippi* was launched on 19 April 1862. However, she was hardly complete. Neither her 20 guns or any ammunition were on board.

Nonetheless, she had admirers in high places. Admiral David Porter called her "The celebrated ram." Her commanding officer, Commander Arthur Sinclair, referred to her as "a formidable ship—the finest of the sort I ever saw in my life; she would, in my opinion, not only have cleared the river of the enemy's vessels, but have raised the blockade of every port in the South." However, her premature deployment up the Mississippi River ended in disaster, as she was fired to prevent capture by forces commanded by Flag Officer David Farragut. The blame for what was perceived as her pointless destruction was at first placed on her builders and then shifted to her commander and finally throughout the Confederate Navy Department with endless hearings that only exposed some of the worst moments of political in-fighting within the department itself.

After the CSS *Virginia, Richmond,* and *Albemarle,* the second CSS *Tennessee* was the most famous. Built on plans drawn by Porter, she had the distinction of being the second of his ships, after *Virginia,* to be commanded by Admiral Franklin Buchanan. Again, Buchanan would take a Porter ironclad against overwhelming odds as he had done with the *Virginia* in March 1862.

Tennessee, a 1,273-ton, 209-feet long ironclad, was built at Selma, Alabama. Carrying her complement of 133 crew members, and a full armament of two 7-inch rifles, and four 6.4-inch rifles, she required a draft of 14-feet.

Laid down in October 1862, her hull and other woodwork were turned out by Henry D. Bassett, who launched her the following February, ready for towing to Mobile where she received her engine and battery. She carried a casemate protected by triple thicknesses of plate that measured 2-inches by 10-inches. A strange addition to her armory was a "hot water attachment to her boilers for repelling boarders, throwing one stream from forward of the casemate and one abaft."

Frustration over her construction schedule quickly grew between Buchanan, Porter and Mallory. Porter wrote in a report published in the *Official Records* that, "The work on the *Tennessee* has progressed for some weeks past, under Mr. Pierce, as fast as the means in his power would permit. There is much delay for want of plate and bolt iron. It was impossible to iron both sponsons at the same time, as the vessel had to be careened several feet to enable them to put the iron on. Even then several of the workmen were waist deep in the water to accomplish it—to careen her, large beams 12 feet square had to be run out of her posts and secured, on which several tons of iron had to be placed, and during the progress of putting on the sponson iron the shield iron could not be put on. The work has been carried on night and day when it could be done advantageously. I visited the *Nashville* and *Tennessee* frequently and, to secure and control the services of the mechanics, I have had them all conscripted and detailed to work under my orders. Previously, they were very independent and stopped working when they pleased."

After her commissioning on 16 February 1864, she was finally towed to Mobile and fitted out for action with Buchanan in command. On August 5, 1864, *Tennessee*, accompanied by wooden gunboats CSS *Gaines, Morgan*, and *Selma* steamed into combat with Federal forces under command of Admiral David G. Farragut. Farragut's fleet consisted of four ironclad monitors and 14 wooden steamers. Unable to use her ram as he had done on *Virginia*, Buchanan ordered a vigorous fire on the Federals at close range. Meanwhile, *Tennessee*'s smaller wooden escorts were either sunk or driven away. Farragut then pulled away and anchored with Buchanan in pursuit, although the Confederate ironclad was outnumbered and outgunned. *Tennessee* soon found herself in a trap as Farragut's entire fleet directed their guns upon her. After being rammed and battered by continuous fire, the rebel ironclad lost her steering chains. Finally after two of her crew were killed and eight wounded including Buchanan, *Tennessee* surrendered.

CHAPTER FIFTEEN

CSS *Richmond*
The Forgotten Ironclad of Gosport

The CSS *Virginia* had not only captured the attention of the world, but brought terror, confusion, and anger to Washington and the White House. Following the Battle of Hampton Roads, President Abraham Lincoln began to personally focus on Gosport. By May 1862, he was directly pressing reluctant Federal forces at Fort Monroe to recapture Norfolk, Portsmouth and the Gosport shipyard at all costs.

The reason for Lincoln's anxiety over Gosport was two-fold. Besides denying the *Virginia* her base of operations, information had reached the White House that Porter was just days from completing a second, and potentially more dangerous ironclad-the CSS *Richmond*.

Even though most in the North concentrated on the *Virginia* as their principal target on the Elizabeth, many in Portsmouth and throughout the South had Porter's second ironclad-the CSS *Richmond*-in mind to permanently break the strangle hold of blockading ships that Lincoln had placed around the Virginia coast.

On the other hand, no one was more eager to get her into action than Porter. After a post-battle inspection of CSS *Virginia*, he knew firsthand the power of the *Monitor* and her consorts. CSS *Richmond*, he decided, had to be designed without the flaws of the converted *Virginia*. From the 90 or so impressions made on the *Virginia*'s shield, including some twenty from the *Monitor*,

107

Porter also knew that the Confederacy's new ironclad had to be stronger to withstand the concentrated fire that was dramatically showing on its predecessor's shield. It also had to be more maneuverable since the *Monitor* required half the time as her more cumbersome opponent to make a complete turn. Since the *Virginia* could make only seven or eight knots on her best day, and left her first ram imbedded in the broken timbers of the *Cumberland* when her engines almost failed to remove her from the sinking warship, Porter knew that the *Richmond* had to have superior machinery over the *Virginia*. The lessons of the Battle of Hampton Roads had been costly, but now Porter planned on implementing his "lessons learned."

As Porter began to make the necessary plans for the CSS *Richmond*, the shortages of iron and other critical building materials came back to haunt him as they had done during the *Virginia* construction. Supplies were difficult to coerce from the Confederate army in 1861, but the situation had become critical by March 1862 when Porter was ready to build. Confederate supply officers simply did not have any iron to spare for a project as obviously critical as a second rebel ironclad in Hampton Roads. For a time it looked as though the *Richmond* was doomed to remain on the drawing board, but the fame of the ironclad *Virginia* saved the day.

When the word spread from Gosport that Porter and his construction crews were out of materials, citizens in Portsmouth and Norfolk organized a public solicitation for money to continue the project. The *Virginia* needed a sister warship, they declared, and she would have one no matter what the costs. Money soon began to pour into the shipyard from across Virginia, and then North Carolina and finally throughout the South. Local newspapers took up the fundraising campaign supporting efforts to build a *New Virginia, Virginia No. 2* or *Young Virginia* as *Richmond* was called before her christening.

However Porter needed iron more than money and this time he could not rely on Tredegar Iron Works in Richmond which was then committed to turning out munitions rather than iron plates like they had made for the *Virginia*. In response to the shortage, local supporters banded together to start a scrap metal collection to build the ship. Any iron object that was not in use was thrown on the shipyard's scrap metal wagons and train cars that passed throughout the state. One wag has it "that many a griddle and iron pot were thrown into those wagons before mamma knew where they had gone!"

By the end of March, Porter had his iron and money. Already highly experienced from the *Virginia*'s conversion project, Gosport's workforce volunteered to labor through the night to get the ship finished. Daily rumors that Federal forces were about to retake Norfolk no doubt spurred Porter and his men onward. Mrs. A.P. Bailey, Porter's granddaughter, said, "During those months he ate breakfast, lunch, and dinner at the shipyard. The only real peace and quiet he had was during his solitary walk home, usually very late in the evening."

Porter was indeed keenly aware of Lincoln's plan to retake Gosport as reliable reports reached Gosport that the President himself was preparing to leave Washington for Fort Monroe and personally direct the attack. Hearing that the *Richmond* was near completion, authorities in the Confederate capital began to badger Porter to release the ship so she could be used to defend Richmond once Hampton Roads fell. Porter knew however that only a few more days were needed to finally have the Richmond ready for its trip to Richmond.

Once again, Gosport's commander began to receive a series of very urgent messages from Mallory in Richmond, who must have had some knowledge of Porter's success at overcoming the shortages of iron that were promised during the construction from the Confederate capital. These messages, contained in the *Official Records,* were sent on April 22, 23, and 24, 1862 and again, most assuredly, frustrated the shipyard commander, Captain Lee and Porter tremendously.

The April 22nd letter:

"Sir: The safety of Norfolk depends, in my judgement, upon the immediate completion of the *Richmond.* The *Virginia* must soon be withdrawn, and the *Monitor* must be opposed by the *Richmond* or nothing. Every available mechanic must therefore be used to complete her, and men must be organized in night gangs in order that there may be no cessation to the work. Commander Rootes will carry one hundred additional workmen to you in a day or two, but in the meantime you can organize a night gang to work by lanterns or otherwise. Mr. Porter thought, when I spoke to him about this plan, that the men could not work at night, but this idea is fallacious, and a separate gang of men must work at night."

Although there is strong evidence that Mallory was unable and perhaps unwilling to spare more iron for the project, his order to Lee on April 23, 1862, contains evidence that indeed some iron was available to complete the project. One can only imagine Porter's expression when he heard from Captain Lee that Mallory was placing the defense of the Norfolk area squarely on his shoulders. The following correspondence from the Confederate Secretary of Navy is found in the *Official Records.*

"Sir: I have already expressed to you my opinion that the safety of Norfolk depends somewhat upon the early completion of the *Richmond,* and I desire that you will make the same confidential communication to Constructor Porter, and urge him to extraordinary exertions by day and night.

"I trust that a hundred extra hands will reach you to-morrow or next day from Fredericksburg with Commander Rootes. The iron will be sent down rapidly, and when the shield shall be ready for it, put as many men upon it as can work, and it may all be put on in twenty-four hours. By a very simple arrangement (a view of which I enclose) a great deal of time will be saved in putting it on."

Perhaps nothing so disturbed Porter in the orders from Mallory as the Secretary's suggestion that Gosport workmen be demanded to work both night and day. Porter argued that night work simply wasn't necessary to get the *Richmond* ready. He also strongly suggested the danger of long hours and the negative effect it would have on the spirit of what he knew was an already overworked shipyard. Porter further stated that night work could cause serious safety problems and possibly cause serious injuries to his men. Nonetheless, Mallory pressed Lee to work around the clock in another order contained in the *Official Records.*

"Sir: You think that the yard would be endangered by fire were men to work at night upon the *Richmond,* and you say that candles or open lamps would have to be used.

"You will of course understand that both the inconvenience

and the risk of night work have been duly considered, and that it is a conviction of its necessity alone dictates the order. Therefore, if you can keep as many men at work upon her in the daytime as can work advantageously, and can, in addition, find a sufficient number of mechanics to form a separate gang for night service, you will so organize and push on the work. With an overwhelming force at your doors, and the prospect of losing Norfolk within twenty days distinctly before us, it will not do to limit the work upon this vessel to one-half this available time. If you can not get men to work at night upon any terms, of course we must lay upon our oars one-half our time; but I think you will be able to find lanterns and to organize a corps of men, boys, or girls even, to hold them and thus enable the mechanics to work at night..."

Both Porter and Lee ignored Mallory's idea about enlisting children. When the yard mechanics heard about Mallory's outlandish request, all volunteered to work as long as Porter needed them to get *Richmond* ready.

The race between Lincoln's planned recapture of Hampton Roads and Porter's *Richmond* came down to the wire. Finally on 6 May 1862 she was prepared. Because of the imminent landings of Federal forces at Ocean View in Norfolk, Virginia, *Richmond* entered the Elizabeth River that night without any fanfare.

Porter had made good his commitment to build a superior ironclad. She measured 150 feet in length, supported a beam of 34 feet and carried a depth of 14 feet. Her draft was half that of the *Virginia*'s 21 feet as *Richmond* required only 12 feet. Her shallow draft made her highly maneuverable over the shallows of the James. *Richmond*'s 150-man crew was provided with two rifled guns on each side, capable of firing solid shot and two shell guns on each side. Much to Porter's approval, she was also equipped with one spar torpedo instead of a ram like the *Virginia*'s. Her shield consisted of 4 inches of iron and 22 inches of yellow pine, but this time because the local iron collection effort gave him sufficient material, he ran the armor plating 3 1/2 feet below her waterline. On the other hand, *Virginia* rose in the water as she depleted her coal and ammunition exposing the original wooden hull of the former USS *Merrimac(k)*. Her lower profile and her more efficient engines gave her distinct advantages over the *Virginia* as well.

John L. Porter

Once Federal forces recaptured Norfolk and Portsmouth, *Richmond* was already well up the James and preparing for the defense of her namesake city. During subsequent battles at Dutch Gap, Fort Harrison, and Chapin's Bluff, Federal shells bounced harmlessly off her sides. Her final day came just prior to the capital's evacuation, April 3, 1865, when she was destroyed to prevent capture.

CHAPTER SIXTEEN

A Hotbed of Politics

Once Porter arrived in downtown Richmond and took his office at the Navy Department on Main Street, he found the capital as he knew he would, a "hotbed of politics." To avoid some of the influence that daily flooded the halls of the department, Porter quietly established another office at Rocketts shipyard along the banks of the James. Here he could work without having to worry about the constant demands of Secretary of Navy Mallory and ignore any developing political intrigues that were generated from the Secretary's office. However in the sweltering summer of 1862, the political storm surrounding Mallory and his "personalized" way of running the Navy Department began to build tremendously. The Confederate Congress itself began to wonder just how effective Mallory was at running the department.

Almost four months after the CSS *Virginia* was destroyed and Gosport evacuated, the Confederate Congress ordered John L. Porter to appear before a broader inquiry on his department's operations. Called an "Investigation of the Navy Department," it was an attempt by the civilian leadership of the Confederacy to provide better oversight of the Navy Department's activities and financial dealings throughout the Confederacy as well as abroad.

The *Official Records* describe the purpose of the inquiry in a joint resolution the Confederate House of Representatives adopted on 27 August 1862. "Resolved by Congress of the Confederate States of America, that a joint select committee of five on the part of the Senate and five on the part of the House be appointed to investigate the administration of the Navy Department under its present head (Stephen Mallory), with power to send for persons and papers, and to report the results of said investigation to the two Houses, respectively."

The minute Porter heard about the investigation, he must have certainly known he would also be called as a primary witness. No doubt this event reminded him of his time before the U.S. Navy inquiry after the fall of Pensacola shipyard two years earlier. Just like his first experience in providing official testimony, Porter was well prepared to give straight forward answers. Some of those answers most certainly annoyed Secretary Mallory, however, there is nothing in the following dialogue that reveals any personal hostility toward the Confederate Secretary of Navy. On a professional level, however, Porter did reveal some doubt about Mallory's policies. In the *Official Records* are found the following sequence of questions and answers during the Confederate Congressional Investigation of the Navy Department. They offer an interesting summary of Porter's career thus far as a Confederate naval constructor and his evaluation of how matters were handled in Richmond.

Tuesday, March 3, 1863
The committee met at 10 o'clock.
Present: Messrs. Clay (chairman), Semmes, Foote, Maxwell, Dupre, Boyce, Barksdale, Peyton, and Phelan.
Mr. John L. Porter having been duly sworn, the following questions were put to him by the Chair on behalf of the Secretary of the Navy:

1st Question. State your name and position in the Navy, and how long you have held this position.
Mr. Porter. My name is John L. Porter; my position is naval constructor. I have served in that capacity in the United States Navy and Confederate States Navy six years.
2nd Question. Have you any knowledge of the course pursued by the Secretary to expedite work under your direction, with reference to working at night and on Sundays?

Mr. Porter. Yes, sir. The orders of the Secretary were very urgent with regard to working on Sundays and at nights. We worked frequently all night whenever we could do so to advantage, and we received orders almost daily from the department urging the necessity of completing the work with all possible dispatch. We did everything that could be done, in fact, to push it forward, and I might say the Secretary required almost impossibilities in the way of executing the work.

Mr. Semmes. Please state what work you allude to.

Mr. Porter. We were altering the *Merrimack* and were fitting out a number of gunboats out of steamers that were brought for the North Carolina service. We were building other ironclad vessels and three wooden gunboats. Two of the wooden boats are in the James River and one we burned at the evacuation of Norfolk. We were doing a great deal of work for the defenses around Norfolk in the way of arms, as a matter of convenience for the batteries, fortifications, etc.

Mr. Semmes. You speak, then, exclusively of the works at Norfolk?

Mr. Porter. Yes, sir.

3rd Question. What duties have you been performing under the Secretary's orders?

Mr. Porter. My duties have been various. I had charge of the operations at the Norfolk Navy Yard up to the time of the evacuation. I made all the drawings, nearly, for the gunboats that were being built in different places. Since the evacuation I have been on duty here in Richmond, carrying on in the yard at Rocketts. I also made a great many plans for the Secretary of the Navy. I have examined several claims of persons against the Navy Department for boats that have been destroyed by the enemy, and have invariably settled them. I have examined a great many plans submitted by persons for gunboats and other purposes. I have been frequently sent out by the Secretary of the Navy to make a general supervision of all works that were in progress for the department. I have been to Savannah, Charleston, Selma, and, in fact, every place that gunboats had been built. I have just returned the week before last after an absence of five weeks, examining boats that were built in different places. We have now

John L. Porter

23 gunboats in course of construction in the Confederacy, 20 ironclads, and 3 wooden boats.

4th Question. In the performance of your duties generally, what has been the course of the Secretary with regard to conducting work promptly and energetically?

Mr. Porter. The Secretary has furnished all possible means and done everything within his power to push work ahead. He has put us in possession of everything essential to the work that it was possible to obtain. If we held Norfolk thirty more days, we would have the *Richmond* completed. We were on the eve of sending a large amount of iron from Richmond, and a large quantity was about being sent from Atlanta. The Secretary had five or six light-draft ironclads being built outside of the navy yard by persons from Norfolk.

5th Question. Was, or was not, the Norfolk yard worked up to its capacity? State the manner of conducting the work there.

Mr. Porter. The yard was worked up to its fullest capacity. In the commencement of our operations we did not do much up to the 1st of July; but after that the yard was worked up to its fullest capacity. Everything was properly organized and the officers were constantly on the spit directing operations and pushing forward the work. The Secretary, in order to stimulate the operations, offered them inducements in the way of additional pay or rewards to work after dark and on Sundays. In short, he offered them every encouragement that was calculated to excite them to more zeal and energy.

Mr. Semmes. How long have you been on duty since the evacuation of Norfolk in the manner I have stated.

Mr. Porter. I did not receive the appointment of naval constructor from the Secretary until last June.

Mr. Semmes. Were you ever sent out to New Orleans to superintend or carry on the construction of the *Mississippi?*

Mr. Porter. No, sir; I made the drawing for the Messrs. Tift of that vessel. I had nothing more to do with her.

Mr. Semmes. Within what time did you suppose the vessel could be constructed when you made the drawing?

Mr. Porter. I did not think she could have been completed in less than nine months, at least. I did not think that a large vessel of her size could be built in a shorter time.

A Hotbed of Politics

Mr. Dupre. What was the condition of Norfolk at the time of its evacuation? Was it in a condition to make a formidable defense?

Mr. Porter. We all thought it was. We were very much surprised on hearing that the place was to be evacuated. The defenses were of the strongest character, and so great our confidence in them that we had no idea that the city would soon be taken.

Mr. Dupre. Were the defenses of Norfolk, of which you speak, under the control of the military or naval authority?

Mr. Porter. Under the military authority. The Navy Department had planned and constructed most of the batteries, but they were turned over to the military authorities. The guns, carriages, etc., were constructed at the navy yard, as well as all the conveniences about the camps, together with boats, flagstaffs, and everything of that sort."

Porter was excused from any further questions. Instead of returning to his office at the Naval Department, he went to Rocketts yard and resumed work at his drawing table. But daily news that the Union advance on Richmond was inching ever forward up the Peninsula continually interrupted his work. He must have been awfully distracted as he wondered how long he and his family would be safe.

CHAPTER SEVENTEEN

The Long Way Home

By 1864, Porter's optimism began to fade rapidly as critical production areas for natural and manufactured materials needed for ironclad construction were captured. Although they were in a struggle now heavily in the Union's favor, Porter and his Confederate counterparts were still able to produce a considerable ironclad fleet. However, in a report he wrote to Mallory on 1 November 1864 while working in Mobile, Alabama, that listed the current Confederate ironclad construction projects under his supervision, Porter noted how significant critical supplies were becoming. His words, always to the point as contained in the *Official Records,* hid his frustration and disappointment well.

"At Mobile-The large ironclad side-wheel steamer, built under contract by Messrs. Montgomery & Anderson, has not been completed for want of iron armor. There are also at this place two light-draft, double-propeller ironclad steamers, to mount four guns each, which were built under contract with Messrs. Porter and Watson, on the Tombigbee River; but the iron armor to complete these vessels is not at present available. Their machinery is being provided for at the Columbus Naval Iron Works. On the Tombigbee another large size ironclad is in progress, for which an engine has been provided, but the armor is wanting.

"It will be seen that everything has been done to get up an ironclad fleet of vessels which could possibly be done under the

119

circumstances, but in consequence of the loss of our iron and coal regions, with the rolling mill at Atlanta, our supply of iron has been very limited. The mills at Richmond are capable of rolling any quantity, but the material is not on hand, and the amount now necessary to complete vessels already built would be equal to 4,230 tons, as follows:

Tons.

At Richmond, for two vessels..........................575
At Wilmington, for one vessel, 1-inch plate..150
At Charleston, two vessels............................800
At Savannah, two vessels..............................750
At Columbus, one vessel...............................280
At Mobile, three vessels.............................1,250
On the Tombigbee, one vessel........................425
Total...4,230

With much respect, your obedient servant,
John L. Porter,
Chief Constructor, CS Navy

By 1865, Porter had realized, as many other well-informed Southerners, that the South could not hold against the manpower and material strength of the North much longer. He watched as ship after ship was captured, destroyed in combat, or scuttled by its own crew to prevent capture. Federal amphibious actions throughout most of the South had closed most of the important Confederate shipyards capable of building ironclads. Once the Confederacy's Gulf Coast area and the vital Mississippi River beginning with Mobile Bay were under Federal control, defeat was inevitable. At the same time the few southern industrial centers left in the interior were not capable of rolling and punching the iron needed for ironclads and producing the steam engines capable of propelling them. With the fall of Richmond, and the destruction of the South's largest iron mill and factory, Tredegar Iron Works, the production base was all but gone. For Porter and the entire Confederate Navy, what started out as a slow retreat, degenerated into a full scale rout.

The Long Way Home

In his notebook, Porter recorded what must have been the agonizing last moments of his work in the Confederate Navy.

"The last gunboat we built was begun in Wilmington (North Carolina), an ironclad. She was well advanced toward completion, the caulkers being ready, when we heard the news that Fort Fisher was captured. We burned her on the stocks and fell back to Halifax, North Carolina. We had a Yard there; the *Albemarle* was fitted out there and did such important action in the capture of Plymouth (North Carolina).

"I must here relate my adventures more particularly from the capture of Wilmington to the surrender of General Johnston at Greensboro, North Carolina and the surrender of General Lee.

"I had my orders to take all my forces, stores, etc., which I had at Wilmington and to fall back to Halifax on the Roanoke River. I had two small flat boats at the yard and commenced to load them up immediately. By three o'clock, we had them both across the river to the railroad depot. But the army had taken possession of all the trains and I could get no transportation.

"I then detailed twelve men to go to the flats, gave some a furlough, and sent the remainder on the train, ordering Naval Constructor Richard Meads to take charge of them. They went on to Halifax. About sunset, we put out from Wilmington up the North East River, intending to intersect the railroad at the bridge. I sent my tools and storage to Halifax. The weather was cold with a heavy frost at night. We continued up that night until the tide began to ebb. We then landed on the bank and made a fire, cooked something to eat and waited for the tide to turn. We then set out again up the river and reached within four miles of the bridge. We had to stop again on account of the head tide. While we were lying on the bank of the river, and cooking again, we saw a heavy cloud of smoke rise from the bridge. We knew it was on fire, but we were at a loss to know who did it. In a short time, a pontoon boat came drifting along filled with water. I had it caught and put in order. We had it ready for service when the tide turned.

"I did not think it prudent to move again until we knew who burned the bridge. I concluded to stay just there until we found out. I sent two men off to scout the area. They returned having found nothing about who burned the bridge. I ordered the men to bring their things ashore and to prepare to spend the night on the ground. We made a fire and laid all night wrapped in blankets. The Federal troops were firing and yelling all night on the other side of the river and higher up the river, toward the bridge.

"Early the next morning, I took a man and went out to reconnoiter for myself. I came to some trenches our troops had dug and thrown up the night before. They made their rifle pits to keep back the Federals who were attacking. It was our men who had fired the bridge to keep the Federals from crossing.

"I soon returned to our camp and gave the men fifteen minutes to get ready to start. I took two men with axes and scuttled the flats and sunk them. We carried whatever could be carried conveniently. We then proceeded cautiously not knowing in whose hands we might fall. We struck out near the main road, leading toward Fayetteville (North Carolina). We did not go up along the railroad for fear of detection and capture.

"Suddenly, we saw two men on horseback approaching. I had ten men with me. But the horsemen were our own. They told us we were on the wrong road to Halifax, but if we would return a short distance they would set us right. We went back with them and soon saw several horsemen standing in the road before us about 40 yards off. We saw them dismount. They opened fire on us immediately with rifles. We had to take to the woods in a hurry to get out of the way of rifle balls which came whistling amongst us. Then the horsemen went like lightning. Their horses made straight tails, and we did not come up to them until sundown, where they had halted.

"The men who fired on us were Confederates but took us for Yankees crossing the river. We then continued our retreat for several days until we struck the railroad at Magnolia (North Carolina). Along the journey, my feet had become bleeding sore and I had to lose two toe nails.

"When we arrived at Halifax, we commenced work on a gunboat that had already been partly built. But, it seemed once again like hoping against hope. Our national affairs grew worse every day. At this time, I received a letter from Major William P. Williamson (Porter's former associate in the construction of the CSS *Virginia*, Chief Steam Engineer, C.S. Navy) at Richmond. He stated that in his opinion Richmond would soon be evacuated in less than ten days at the most. My family was there, so I started out for there immediately. By the time I reached Raleigh, I learned that Richmond had fallen. President Davis had fallen back to Danville and General Lee to Appomattox Court House (Virginia) where he had surrendered his small force to General Grant."

It must have been heart-wrenching for Porter when he learned that Richmond had fallen. Questions about the fate of his family continually haunted him. His daughter, Martha Buxton Brent, then fifteen, left an eye-witness account of Richmond's collapse and the Confederate withdrawal.

"The second of April, 1865, was a bright sunny day in Richmond," Brent wrote, "but to the people going home from morning service the streets seemed filled with some strange undercurrent of excitement.

"Men walked about talking earnestly and looking very seriously. Before reaching home the secret was revealed. The City was to be evacuated that afternoon, and, after some hours, Mr. Davis (Confederate President Jefferson Davis) and his Cabinet and department clerks left to try to join Lee's Army, taking with them the State papers and the small quantity of gold and silver in the Confederate Treasury.

"The distress of the Richmond people was inexpressible. It was the beginning of the end. I don't think the lights went out in a single house that night. About 11 P.M. the sounds of heavy explosions came to our ears. It was the destruction of the small navy on the James to prevent their capture.

"Men were breaking open the liquor stores on Main Street and emptying the barrels into the gutters to keep it from exciting the invaders and causing them to do harm to the people. The odor filled the lower part of the City.

"Early Monday morning the great fire started somewhere near the river. Who began it, or for what purpose? It was terrible. It swept over the western part of the City and stopped within sight of our home. I went in the early morning with my brother to my father's office on Main Street to save his papers (including the plans of the CSS *Virginia* and related drawings), which we brought home.

"Just across the narrow street two young ladies stood on their porch and talked to my brother. Before twelve o'clock the flames were sweeping down on them so rapidly they rushed out without even saving their clothes. Many Virginia planters had stored their crops in Richmond to prevent their falling into the hands of the enemy's raiding parties. My husband's father had two years' tobacco crop in a warehouse there. It was destroyed by the fire. The fire was put out by the Federal soldiers.

"On Monday morning between 10 and 11, I think, the first Union soldiers entered Richmond. The report was circulated that when the news of the evacuation reached Grant, he called for volunteers to investigate and these seventeen young Cavalrymen volunteered. I saw them riding up Governor Street from Main towards the Capitol and I watched at the windows to see what would happen. A story was in the Richmond papers some time ago to the effect that the Confederate flag flying was torn into pieces and distributed among the Union soldiers. It was a mistake. There was no "Stars and Bars" waving, but the "Sic Semper Tyrannis" of Virginia. It was immediately lowered and replaced by the "Stars and Stripes," a veritable instrument of *stripes* in this case. In an hour or two the Union Army marched into Richmond by the thousands.

"My father was in North Carolina, directing the construction of more ironclads, they were to meet the usual fate of his work, for the South; that is, to be blown up to prevent their falling into the hands of the enemy.

"My mother had carried from the beginning of the war a small buckskin purse, containing ten twenty dollar gold pieces, which she refused to spend for anything. That was our resource in this time of need. Gold was at a premium, so our $200 brought us $250. She succeeded in selling the piano at a fair price and we waited for the end which came on April 9th. Then Lee surrendered to Grant and all was over. There was no cruelty or insult connected with the surrender. Grant allowed our soldiers to take their horses home with them, and the "yanks" divided their food with the "Rebs," in all good nature.

"Then my father's brother, Joseph, wrote from Portsmouth, 'Come home Susan (Porter's wife), the latch hangs out. I can take care of you all.' So we proceeded by the James River Route."

Meanwhile, Porter prepared for the end as well and described his final duties as Chief Naval Constructor, Confederate States Navy, in his notebook.

"I went on to Greensboro and there rented a room and made myself as contented as I could. After General Lee's surrender, the President and cabinet fell back to Greensboro also. General Johnston's forces fell back to Greensboro and everything seemed in a fog. I remained in Greensboro a month. General Johnston saw the cause was lost and made arrangements with General Sherman, who was near Raleigh, to surrender his forces. This was done on the first day of May, 1865."

CHAPTER EIGHTEEN

A True Rendering

Following his surrender and parole on April 28, 1865, at Greensboro, North Carolina, Porter joined other war-weary Confederate veterans and returned home the best way he could. For all his achievements in the Confederate Navy, he now relied on a Federal parole certificate dated 1 May to prove his identity as he passed through the Union infantry checkpoints.

Upon his arrival in Portsmouth on 9 May at his brother Joseph's house, he rejoiced that his family had escaped the battle of Richmond and survived the subsequent evacuation. But he also knew that without a job and already financially ruined, the family's destitution had only begun with the end of the war. Despite everything, the Porters had fared well considering the circumstances.

"Portsmouth had been in the hands of the Federals for three years," Brent wrote, "but little business was going on. Nevertheless the little city managed to feed the returned 'Rebels' until better times. Many citizens had guests. The whole South was ruined. The town was filled with Union soldiers.

"Our old slaves came to see us, showing as much affection as in bygone days. Willis was dead, but when, years later, Matilda passed away, my mother paid her burial expenses. My father soon established us in a home, just after the war, and went to Baltimore, looking for work, which he succeeded in finding."

Porter was shocked and dismayed when he found that former Confederate shipyard workers need not apply at Gosport for

127

employment. Fortunately his youthful interest and training in ship carpentry would pay off once more as it put bread on the table for his family after he found work back in Richmond under a state contract to build three oyster patrol boats, *Tredegar, Wm. F. Taylor* and *Virginia*. A November 25, 1867, article in the Norfolk Journal described Porter's new work. "The three steamers contracted for by the Tredegar Works have been launched and were taken through the locks on Friday to the ship basin, where they will soon be completed. They are said to be beautiful models. They could not have been otherwise, as they were constructed under the supervision of our fellow citizen of Portsmouth, John L. Porter, formerly Constructor in the United States Navy, and more recently in that of the Confederacy.

"These boats are each sixty feet in length, with a beam of thirteen feet and a depth of hold of five and a half feet. The propellers are four bladed and of a diameter of five feet. The horse power is thirty, and they are of forty tons each. The holds are of iron, decks and upper works oak and pine."

Porter's writings at this time are those of a dejected and defeated man. It is obvious that he spared himself some room for introspection. There is clear evidence of some bitterness and disappointment in his words about why he had ever joined with the Confederacy and left what he knew was a bright future with the U.S. Navy.

"When I returned home to Portsmouth, I found that my house had been confiscated and sold to a man named Hustes for $700.00 by the U.S. Marshall, and a deed given him at the close of the War. Everyone seemed out for himself. No one seemed to sympathize with me for the loss of my house.

"I applied for several small offices in the government of the city council, but was given no showing whatsoever. While I was Constructor in the Navy, I had friends a plenty, but after the War, I had none. I was left poor and needy. I often regretted that I ever gave up my situation which had offered me a good living for life. Instead, I had to rough it for a living in the shipyards."

As Brent mentioned earlier, Porter's search for work after the war carried him to Baltimore where, for a time, he served as superintendent of Abrams & Sons shipyard. Later he returned to Portsmouth, and as restrictions on the employment of former

Confederates began to lessen, he accepted a position as ship constructor at the Atlantic Iron Works located in the Berkley section of Norfolk.

During his time at the Atlantic Iron Works, he was often called upon by a number of shipping agents and builders to examine their ships for overhaul or repair. One incident in 1869 described how Porter's talent and ingenuity had not diminished. On November 22 of that year, the *Norfolk Virginian* carried an article about Porter's involvement in repairing the steamer *Ella* that had sunk in North Carolina on the Chowan River. After she was pumped and raised, the *Ella* was taken to Franklin, Virginia where she was met by Porter.

"Mr. Hill, the *Ella's* enterprising agent, engaged the services of John L. Porter, Superintendent of the ship yard department at the Atlantic Iron Works to make the necessary repairs, if possible, without hauling her out of the water, for no suitable marine railway was available.

"Her bottom plank, near the turn of the bilge, had been broken through in two places, making an opening 5 feet in length and 10 inches wide.

"Mr. Porter constructed a large box and without the assistance of a diver fitted it so nicely to the bottom of the steamer, that after Mr. Maxwell, her engineer, had pumped out the water, the workmen went down with the box and repaired the damage as well as if she had been taken on a railway.

"It was a novel scene to the people of Franklin, and many doubted its practicability until after its successful accomplishment, when they complimented Mr. Porter on his skill. The *Ella* will resume her regular trips today."

Literally to make ends meet, Porter offered his services whenever he could to the many small shipyards that were beginning to re-establish themselves along the Elizabeth. In May, 1872, the Norfolk Journal carried an article about his construction of a tugboat for B. & J. Baker Company, the salvagers who had brought the remains of the ironclad *Virginia* back into the shipyard. Christened at Ferry Point in Berkley, between Norfolk and Portsmouth in the Elizabeth River, with a large gathering looking on, the *Nettie*'s one hundred tons burden was described as "a beautiful vessel." By May 1878, Porter had finally returned to

Gosport but this time not as ship constructor as he wrote in his notebook.

"George Boush, United States Naval Constructor, took me in charge of some ship work. I agreed, it was the first kindness I had received from anyone in these parts. Since the close of the war, strange events had happened. I had given him employment many times, when I was in authority-but now the scene changes, he is the constructor. I am derated and have to apply to him for employment as a carpenter. I appreciate Mr. Boush's kindness to me and also Mr. William Smith, the Master Shipwright. May neither of them have such misfortunes as I have had." After serving in the Norfolk Navy Yard (formerly Gosport Shipyard) carpentry shop, Porter was finally recognized for his talents when he was appointed superintendent of ship construction for Baker's Berkley shipyard.

During the late 1870's, Porter had accumulated enough money to bring his family back to one of their ancestral homes. Brent wrote, "My father managed to buy back great-grandfather Pritchard's home on Washington and Glasgow Streets, and we were comfortable once more."

Porter left Baker's shipyard in 1883 to become superintendent of the Norfolk County Ferries. The overall supervision of what was then the oldest continuously operated ferry system in the nation brought him great satisfaction. He not only maintained several of the older steam-driven vessels but designed several new ferries that were in operation well into the 20th century. At his retirement in 1888, he had once again placed his family on firm financial footing.

John L. Porter died on December 14, 1893 and was buried in Cedar Grove Cemetery, less than a mile from where he was born and grew up. In addition to the granite obelisk that marks his grave, a state historical marker commemorating his life stands near the Ferry Boat Landing on Portsmouth's High Street near the site of his last employment.

Now that John L. Porter belongs to the ages, it is important for our nation's history that he be remembered for his outstanding character, love of community and church, and major contributions to naval technology. It is indeed a befitting legacy that modern U.S. Navy warships, still incorporating many of his contributions,

A True Rendering

pass by the Portsmouth waterfront to this day where the first Porters came to build ships in the eighteenth century.

For his accomplishments in warship design and development, he stands among the greats as one of America's most outstanding ship constructors. John L. Porter of Portsmouth was indeed a naval constructor of destiny

BIBLIOGRAPHY

_____,' "The *Merrimack* is Salvaged," *Lynchburg Daily Virginian*, June 13, 1861.

_____, Norfolk Day Book, "An Offer for Plans," November 16, 1861.

_____, Argus, January 17, 1848, The Foundry in Portsmouth.

_____, *The Beacon*, July 26, 1848, Gosport Iron Works.

_____, *Civil War Naval Chronology*, Washington: Naval History Division, Navy Department, 1971.

_____, *Official Records of the Union and Confederate Navies in the War of the Rebellion*, 31 volumes, Washington, DC: Government Printing Office, 1884-1927.

_____, "U.S. Congress, House Report of the Secretary of the Navy in Relation to Ironclad Vessels," Washington: Document 69, 38th Congress, 1st Session, 1863.

_____, *Dictionary of American Biography*, New York, Charles Scribner's & Sons, 1929.

Amadon, George F. *Rise of the Ironclads*, Missoula, MT: Pictorial Histories Publishing Co., 1988.

Barnard, Major J. G. *Notes on Sea Coast Defenses*, New York: Von Norstard, 1861.

Bathe, Greville. *Ship of Destiny, a Record of the Steam Frigate Merrimac, 1855-1862*, Philadelphia: Allen, Lane and Scott, 1951

Baxter, James M. *The Introduction of the Ironclad Warship*, Cambridge: Harvard University press, 1933.

Bennett, Frank M. *The Steam Navy of the United States*, Philadelphia: W. T. Nicholson Press, 1896.

Besse, Sumner B. *C.S. Ironclad Virginia and U.S. Ironclad Monitor*, Newport News: The Mariners Museum, 1937.

Brooke, George M. Jr. *John M. Brooke, Naval Scientist and Educator*, Charlottesville: University of Virginia Press, 1980.

Brooke, John M. Diary entry dated June 23, 1861, Lexington, Virginia: private papers of George M. Brooke.

Brooke, John M. "The Plan and Construction of the *Merrimac*," *Battles and Leaders of the Civil War*, vol. I, New York: The Century Company, 1884-1888.

Brooke, John M. Personal Diary and Private Papers of George M. Brooke, Lexington, Virginia.

Buchanan, Franklin. "Battle between the *Virginia* and *Monitor*," *The Confederate Soldier in the Civil War*, New York: The Fairfax Press, (no date).

Burton, H. W. *History of Norfolk, Virginia, 1736 to 1877*, Norfolk: Private Press, 1877.

Campbell, R. Thomas. *Academy on the James, the Confederate Naval School*, Shippensburg: White Mane Publishing, Inc., 1998.

Campbell, R. Thomas. *Gray Thunder*, Shippensburg: White Mane Publishing Company, Inc., 1996.

Clemmer, Gregg S. *Valor in Gray*, Staunton: The Hearthside Publishing Company, 1996.

Cline, William R. "The Ironclad Ram *Virginia* – Confederate States Navy," *Southern Historical Society Papers*, vol. XXXII.

Coski, John M. *Capital Navy*, Campbell: Savas Woodbury Publishers, 1996.

Craver, Zachariah. Letter to his family, Hampton, Virginia, May 21, 1861.

Current, Richard N. *Encyclopedia of the Confederacy*, New York: Simon & Schuster, 4 volumes, 1993.

Davis, William C. *Jefferson Davis, The Man and His Hour*, New York: Harper Collins Publishers, 1991.

Davis, William C. *Duel Between the First Ironclads*, New York: Doubleday & Company, Inc., 1975.

Donnelly, Ralph W. *The Confederate States Marine Corps*, Shippensburg: White Mane Publishing Company, Inc., 1989.

Durkin, Joseph T. *Confederate Navy Chief: Stephen R. Mallory*, Chapel Hill: The University of North Carolina Press, 1954.

Bibliography

Eggleston, John R. "Captain Eggleston's Narrative of the Battle of the Merrimac," *Southern Historical Society Papers*, vol. XLI, 1916.

Evans, Clement A. (Editor). *Confederate Military History*, Atlanta: Confederate Publishing Company, 1899.

Flanders, Alan B. *Memoirs of E. A. Jack, Steam Engineer, CSS Virginia*, White Stone: Brandylane Publishers, Inc. and the Friends of the Portsmouth Naval Shipyard Museum, 1998.

Flanders, Alan B. *The Merrimac, the Story of the Conversion of the U.S.S. Merrimac into the Confederate Ironclad Warship, C.S.S. Virginia*, Portsmouth: The Portsmouth Naval Shipyard Museum, 1982.

Flanders, Alan B. "The Night They Burned the Yard," *Civil War Times Illustrated*, February, 1980.

Foute, R. C. "Echoes From Hampton Roads," *Southern Historical Society Papers*, vol. XIX, 1891.

Isherwood, B. F. *Experimental Researches in Steam Engineering*, Philadelphia: (publisher unknown), vol. I, 1863.

Jones, Catesby ap R. Personal Letters and Private Papers, Lexington, Virginia.

Jones, Catesby ap R. "Services of the *Virginia (Merrimac)*," *Southern Historical Society Papers*, vol. XI, 1883.

Jones, Virgil C. *The Civil War at Sea*, 3 volumes, New York: Holt, Rinehart, and Winston, 1960-1962.

Lewis, Charles Lee. *Admiral Franklin Buchanan; Fearless man of Action*, Baltimore: The Norman Remington Company, 1929.

Lewis, John H. *Recollections from 1860 to 1865*, Washington: Peake & Company, 1895.

Long, John S. "The Gosport Affair, 1861," *Journal of Southern History*, May, 1957.

Lull, Edward P. *History of the United States Navy Yard at Gosport Virginia*, Washington: Government Printing Office, 1874.

Luraghi, Raimondo. *History of the Confederate Navy*, Annapolis: Naval Institute Press, 1996.

Melton, Maurice. *The Confederate Ironclads*, New York: Thomas Yoseloff, Ltd., 1968.

Moebs, Thomas T. *Confederate States Navy Research Guide*, Williamsburg: Moebs Publishing Company, 1991.

Newton, Virginius. "The Ram Merrimac," *Southern Historical Society Papers*, vol. XX, 1892.

Norris, William. "The Story of the Confederate States Ship *Virginia*," *Southern Historical Society Papers*, vol. XLII, 1879.

Page, David. *Ships Versus Shore*, Nashville: Rutledge Hill Press, 1994.

Parker, William H. *Recollections of a Naval Officer*, New York: Charles Scribners' Sons, 1883.

Peters, William H. *Recollections of Facts and Circumstances Connected With the Evacuation of the Navy Yard at Portsmouth, Virginia, April, 1861.*

Porter, John L. *The CSS Virginia. The Story of her Construction and Battle*, Portsmouth: Portsmouth Naval Shipyard Museum, Marshal W. Butt Library.

Porter, John L. *A Short History of Myself*, Portsmouth: Portsmouth Naval Shipyard Museum, (Porter Letter book).

Porter, John W. H. "The *Virginia* or *Merrimac*, Her Real Projector," *Southern Historical Society Papers*, vol. XIX, 1891.

Porter, John W. H. "Origin of an Ironclad," *Confederate Veteran*, May, 1915.

Ramsay, Ashton. "Wonderful Career of the *Merrimac*," *Confederate Veteran*, 1907.

Ramsay, Ashton. "Most Famous of Sea Duels: The *Merrimac* and *Monitor*," *Harpers Weekly*, vol. LVI, 1907.

Rodgers, C. R. P. *History of the United States Navy Yard at Gosport, Virginia*, Washington: Government Printing Office, 1874

Rochelle, James H. "The Confederate Steamship Patrick Henry," *Southern Historical Society Papers*, vol. XIV, 1896.

Scharf, J. Thomas. *History of the Confederate States Navy,* New York: Crown Publishers, Inc., 1877.

Shingleton, Royce Gordon. *John Taylor Wood, Sea Ghost of the Confederacy*, Athens: University of Georgia Press, 1979.

Silverstone, Paul H. *Warships of the Civil War Navies,* Annapolis: Naval Institute Press, 1989.

Bibliography

Stern, Philip Van Doren. *The Confederate Navy, A Pictorial History*, New York: Bonanza Books, 1962.

Still, Jr., William N. *Iron Afloat*, Nashville: Vanderbilt University Press, 1971.

Still, Jr., William N. *Confederate Shipbuilding*, Columbia: University of South Carolina Press, 1969.

Still, Jr., William N. *The Confederate Navy, The Ships, Men and Organization, 1861-65*, Annapolis: Naval Institute Press, 1997.

Tindale, William. "The True Story of the Virginia and the Monitor," *The Virginia Magazine of History and Biography*, vol. XXXI, January, 1923.

Wells, Tom H. *The Confederate Navy, A Study in Organization*, Birmingham: The University of Alabama Press, 1971.

Wertenbaker, Thomas J. *Norfolk: Historic Southern Port*, Durham: Duke University Press, 1931.

Williamson, Thomas. *Family Memoirs*, Blair private papers.

Wingfield, J. H. D. "A Thanksgiving Service on the *Virginia*, March 10, 1862," *Southern Historical Society Papers*, vol. XIX.

Wood, John Taylor. "The First Fight of Iron-clads," *Battles and Leaders of the Civil War*, vol. I, New York: The Century Company, 1884-1888.

INDEX

Albemarle, CSS 102, 103, 104, 121
Albion 23, 28
Alert 23
Allegheny, USS 7, 9, 38
anti-secessionist *See* secessionist
Armstrong, James, Commodore 29–35, 42
Atlantic Iron Works 129
Baker's shipyard 130
Battle of Hampton Roads 89, 90, 107, 108
Battle of Mobile Bay 29
Baxter, James M. 7, 8
Ben Franklin 19
Brandywine, USS 41
Brent, Martha Buxton Porter 3–7, 11, 12, 19–27, 123, 128, 130
Brooke, John M., Lieutenant 50, 55, 56, 60, 63–67, 73–80
Buchanan, Franklin, Commodore 58, 68–71, 92, 93, 96, 104, 105
Buxton, James 4
Charleston 28
Charleston, South Carolina 23, 28, 102, 115, 120
Chicora, CSS 102
Civil War 4–11, 21–31, 49, 103
Colorado, USS 15, 21, 22, 38, 50
Columbia, USS 21, 44, 46
Columbus Naval Iron Works 119, 120
Columbus, USS 41, 44, 45
Confederate States, CSS 42. *See also* USS *United States*
Confederate States Navy 48, 50, 54, 59, 66, 75, 79, 114, 125
Congress, USS 23, 68, 90, 91, 92
Constellation, USS 13, 15, 16, 17, 18, 38
Constitution, USS 16
Cumberland, USS 23, 41–47, 68, 85, 91–93, 108

Daily Southern Argus 15, 17
Dale, Richard, Commodore x
Delaware, USS 2, 41, 44, 45
Denbigh 29
Dolphin, USS 44, 45, 46
Dyson, William 1, 2
Elizabeth, CSS 102
Elizabeth River x, 1, 3, 4, 10, 18, 19, 42, 46, 61, 97, 107, 111, 129
Ella, USS 129
Elliott, Gilbert 99, 102
Escambia, CSS 102
Fairfax, A. B., Commander 61, 68
Farmer, James 57
Farragut, David G., Admiral 104, 105
Forrest, French, Commodore 39, 48, 59, 60, 66, 75, 78, 95, 100
Fortress Monroe 69, 70, 89, 90–95
Fox, Josiah 2, 16
Fredericksburg, CSS 2, 103
Gaines, CSS 105
Germantown, USS 41, 42, 44, 45, 46
Gosport Navy Yard. *See* Gosport shipyard
Gosport shipyard xi, 1–4, 11, 15–28, 37–63, 74, 82, 83, 87, 89–103, 107–113, 127, 130
Grice, Francis 2
Hampton, CSS 101
Hampton Roads, battle of 89, 90, 107, 108
Hampton Roads, Virginia 4, 9, 19, 23, 28, 49, 58, 63, 69, 73, 89–99, 108–111
Harmony 28
Harriet Lane 44
Hartt, Samuel 15, 16, 18, 21
High Street, Portsmouth 81
Hodges, Matilda 25
Hodges, Willis 12, 13, 20
Humphreys, Joshua 2, 16

139

Hunter, William W., Lieutenant 4, 7, 8, 9, 50
Indian Chief 1
ironclad vessel ix, 7, 8, 21–23, 28, 49–59, 63–79, 89–97, 105
Jamestown, CSS 92
Jarvis, John 16, 17
Jones, Catesby ap, Lieutenant 25, 61, 68, 69, 93
Josephine 29
Justice, author of a news article 73, 74
La Gloire 22, 49
Lackawana, USS 29
Lambell, William 2
Le Grand 25
Lee, Sidney S., Captain 61, 68, 95, 97, 109–111
Lincoln, Abraham 31, 107
Luke, Elizabeth x
Luke, Isaac x
Magruder, John B., General 44, 95, 96
Mallory, Stephen R. 48–66, 74–80, 95, 97, 100, 104, 109–114, 119
Mary 22
McCauley, Charles S., Commodore 37–47, 50
Meads, James 57–60, 66
Meads, Richard 121
mechanics 4, 10, 34, 60, 101, 105, 111
Merrimac(k), USS 7, 8, 21, 23, 41–47, 50, 51, 56,–71, 73, 80, 83, 84, 85, 89–95, 111, 115
Minnesota, USS 68, 92, 93
Mississippi, CSS 15, 103, 104, 116
Mobile Bay, battle of 29
Monitor, USS 23, 64, 69, 70, 86, 89–95, 107–109
Monumental Methodist Church, Portsmouth 81
Moore, Reverend 86
Morgan, CSS 105
Nansemond, CSS 101
Nashville, CSS 105
naval constructor 2, 9, 15, 16, 29–38, 47, 48, 59, 63–65, 80, 90, 95, 99, 121, 125, 130, 131

Nettie 129
Neuse, CSS 103
New York 46
New York Navy Yard 28
Norfolk County Ferries 130
Norfolk, CSS 101
Norfolk Navy Yard 65, 75, 82, 103, 115, 130. *See also* Gosport shipyard
Norfolk, Virginia 1,–12, 18, 19, 28, 41–50, 77, 100, 107–117, 129
North Carolina, CSS 102
Official Records 32, 59, 96, 100, 105, 109, 110, 113, 114, 119
"Old Ironsides" 22
Palmetto State, CSS 102
Parrish, Captain 70, 92
Pawnee, USS 32, 37, 41, 45–47
Pennsylvania, USS 17, 41, 44–47, 82
Pensacola, Florida 25, 27, 29–33
Pensacola Naval Station 32
Pensacola Navy Yard 25, 26, 31
Pensacola, USS 32
Peters, William H. 42, 43, 45, 48
Pittsburgh, Pennsylvania 7–10, 53–55, 64
Plymouth, North Carolina 102, 121
Plymouth, USS 41, 43–46
Porpoise, USS 41
Porter, Alice 4, 27
Porter, Angelina 2
Porter, Caroline 1
Porter, Emily 1
Porter, Fletcher 1, 3
Porter, George 11, 25, 26, 54
Porter, John, Jr. xi
Porter, John Luke ix, 1–3, 20, 28, 54, 63–65, 76, 79, 95, 113, 114, 120, 128–131
Porter, John W.H. 4, 8, 43, 46, 48, 53–61
Porter, Joseph x, xi
Porter, Joseph H. 3, 10, 11, 60, 127
Porter, Joseph, II 1, 2, 3
Porter, Mary Buxton. *See* Brent, Martha Buxton Porter

Index

Porter, Mary Susan 4, 11, 27
Porter, Samuel xi
Porter, Samuel, Jr. xi
Porter shipyard 1, 2
Porter, Sidney 1, 4
Porter, Virginia 1
Porter, William xi, 1, 12
Porter, William, Jr. x, xi
Portsmouth, Virginia ix, x, 1–3, 9–23, 26–29, 37–47, 50, 56, 61, 81, 82, 87, 97, 102, 107, 108, 112, 124–131
Potomac, USS 15, 41
Powhatan, USS 15
Raleigh, CSS 102
Raritan, USS 15, 44, 46
Rebecca 25, 26
Richmond, CSS 101–104, 107–112, 116
Richmond Enquirer 73, 74
Richmond Examiner 74, 76
Roanoke, USS 15, 22, 23
Rocketts shipyard 113
Savannah, CSS 102
Savannah, Georgia 102, 115, 120
secession 30–38, 50
secessionists 31–38
Selma, Alabama 104, 115
Selma, CSS 105
Seminole, USS 27, 28, 29, 38
Sidney, John, Colonel xi
Sidney, Mary xi
Sir William Peel, HMS 28
slaves 5, 11, 12, 25, 31, 127
steam frigates 21, 22
steam power 1, 2, 4, 7, 16, 21, 22, 38, 50, 64, 120
Tattnall, Josiah, Captain 69, 70, 89, 90, 94, 95
Teaser, CSS 92
Tennessee, CSS 29, 104, 105
Thomas Watson 23
Tomlinson shipyard 9
Tredegar 128
Tredegar Iron Works 60, 67, 108, 120, 128

United States Navy 3, 7, 8, 21, 29–31, 38–43, 48, 54, 90, 102, 114, 128
United States, USS 41, 44
Virginia, CSS ix, 8, 21, 23, 27, 28, 47, 51, 58–64, 70–79, 84, 85, 86, 89–97, 101–113, 122–129. *See also Merrimac(k)*, USS
War of 1812 ix
Warrior, HMS 22, 49
Washington Naval Yard 32, 37
Whig 73, 74
Williamson, William P., Major 50–59, 64–66, 73–79, 99–101, 122
Wm. F Taylor, CSS 128
Wool, General 89, 94
Worden, John L., Admiral 70, 93, 95
Yadkin, CSS 102
yellow fever 18, 19, 20

141